Coloring for Life: Colorful Coast Long Beach Island Edition

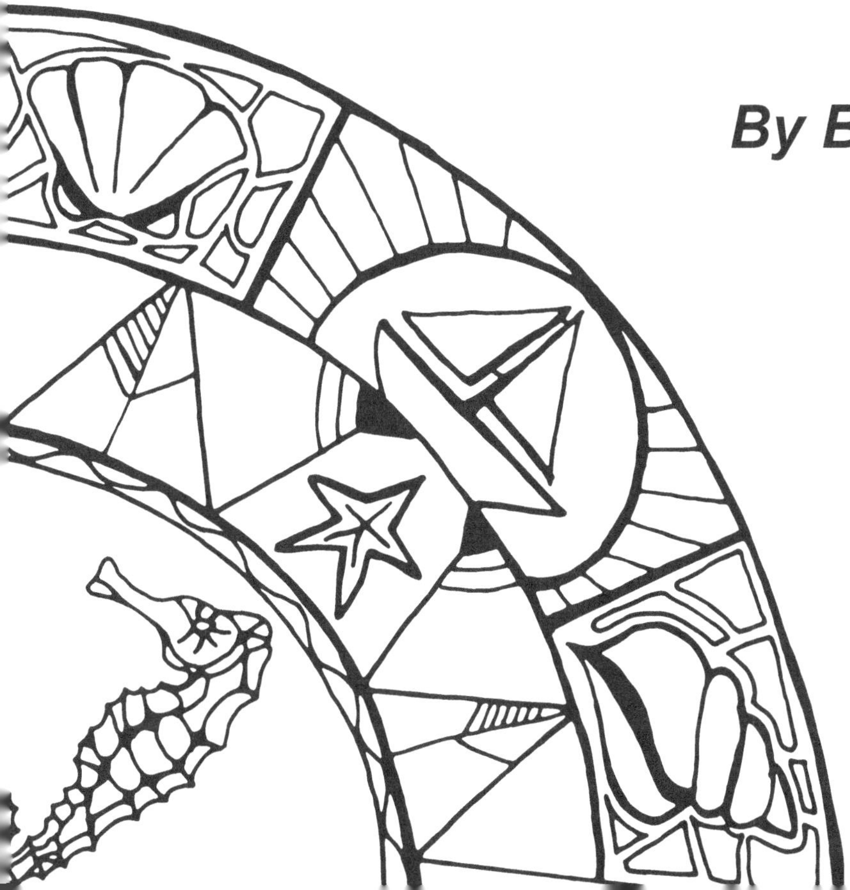

By Bill Clanton

ISBN-13:
978-0-9974996-3-6

ISBN-10:
099749963X

Introduction

The Colorful Coast: Long Beach Island Edition incorporates some images and themes from the Long Beach Island region of New Jersey. At its core, Colorful Coast is an adult coloring book or coloring book for grown ups that captures the excitement of a day at the beach and puts it on the pages for you to color. Color fun mosaics and mandalas as well as sketched art, abstract nautical images, and underwater sea life. This book is the perfect companion for your next beach day under the umbrella, a day out on the boat, or just letting the stresses of the day melt away as you dream of a day at the beach.

Sign up for our newsletter at coloringforlife.com and receive free coloring pages and updates on future Coloring for Life coloring books.

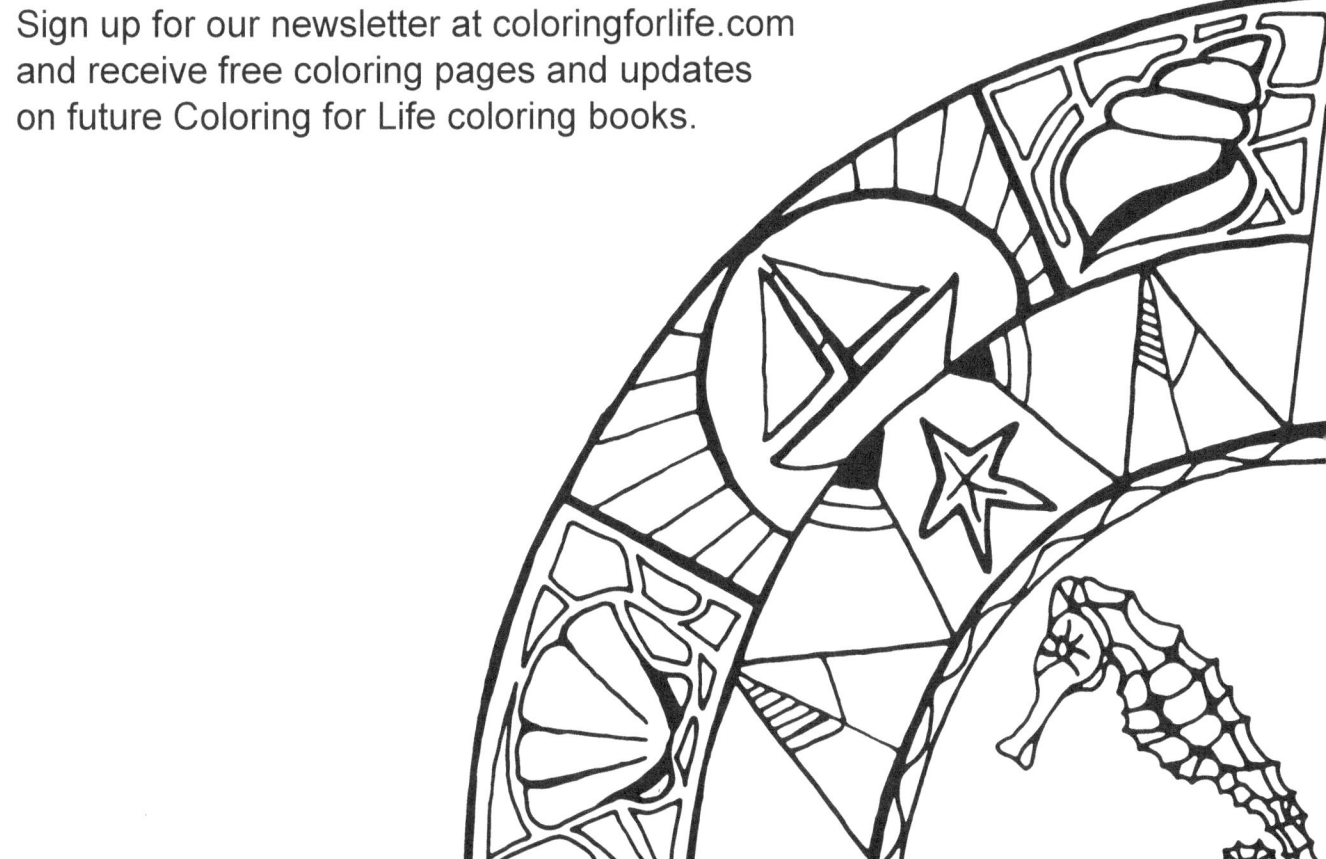

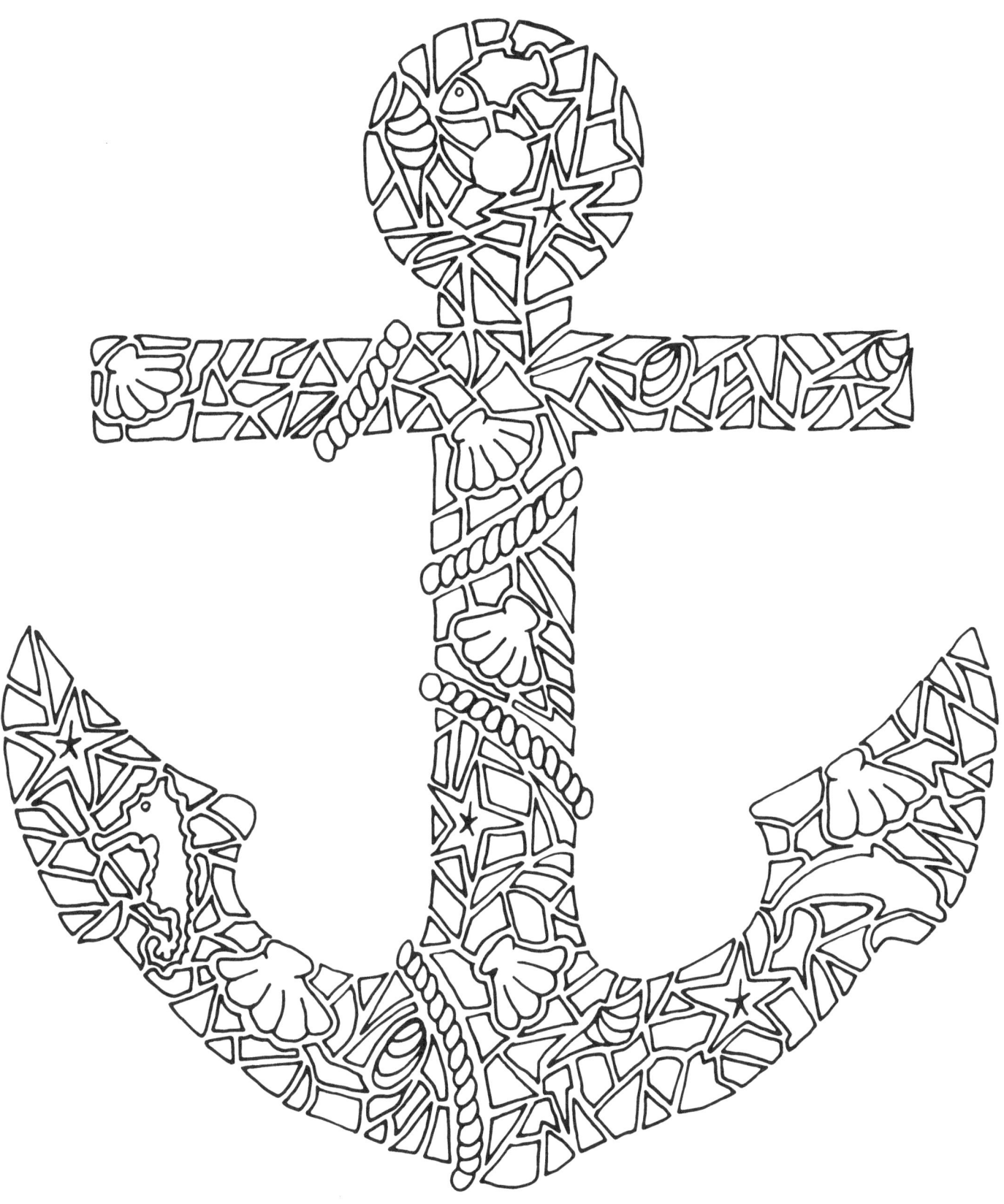

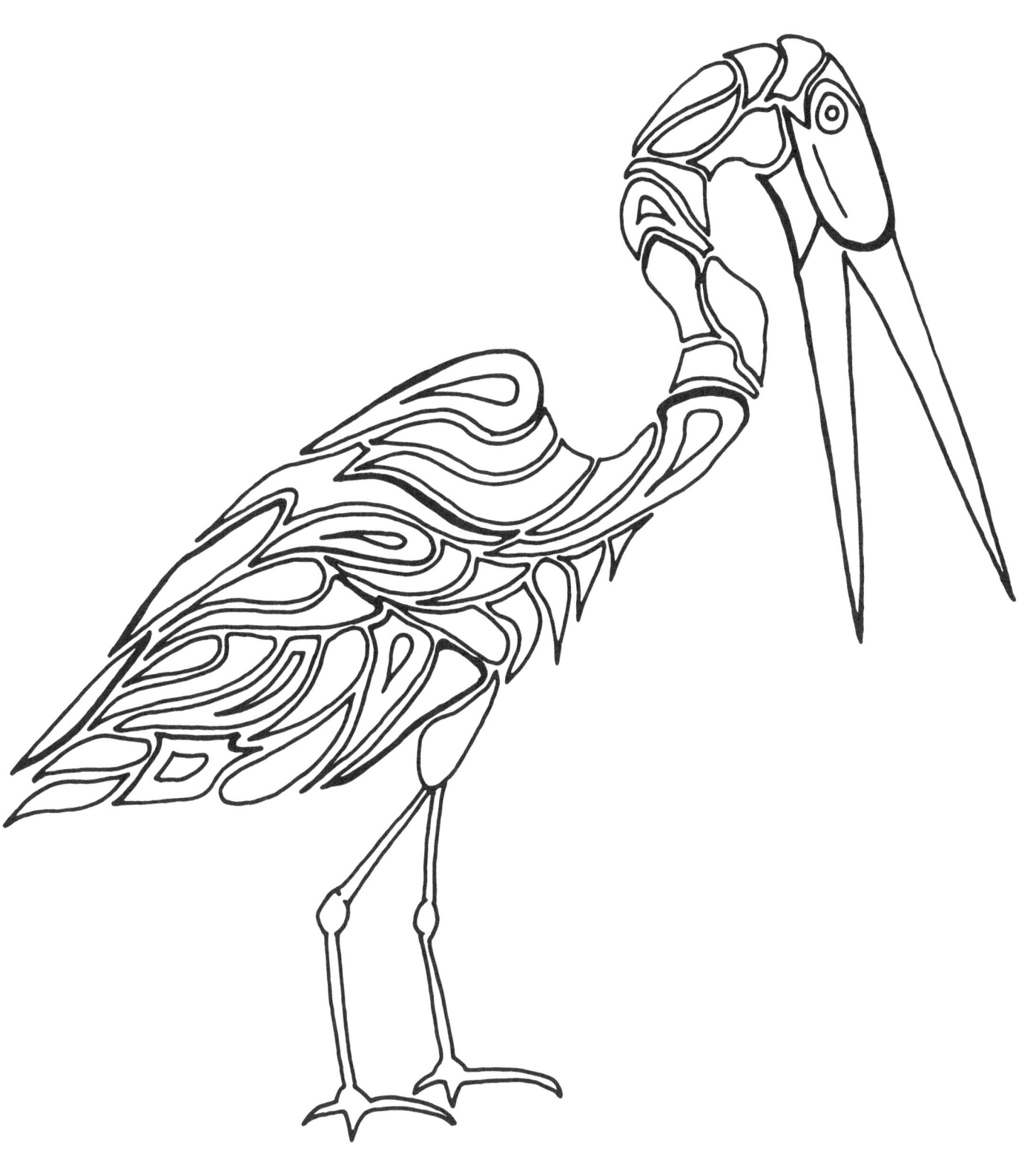

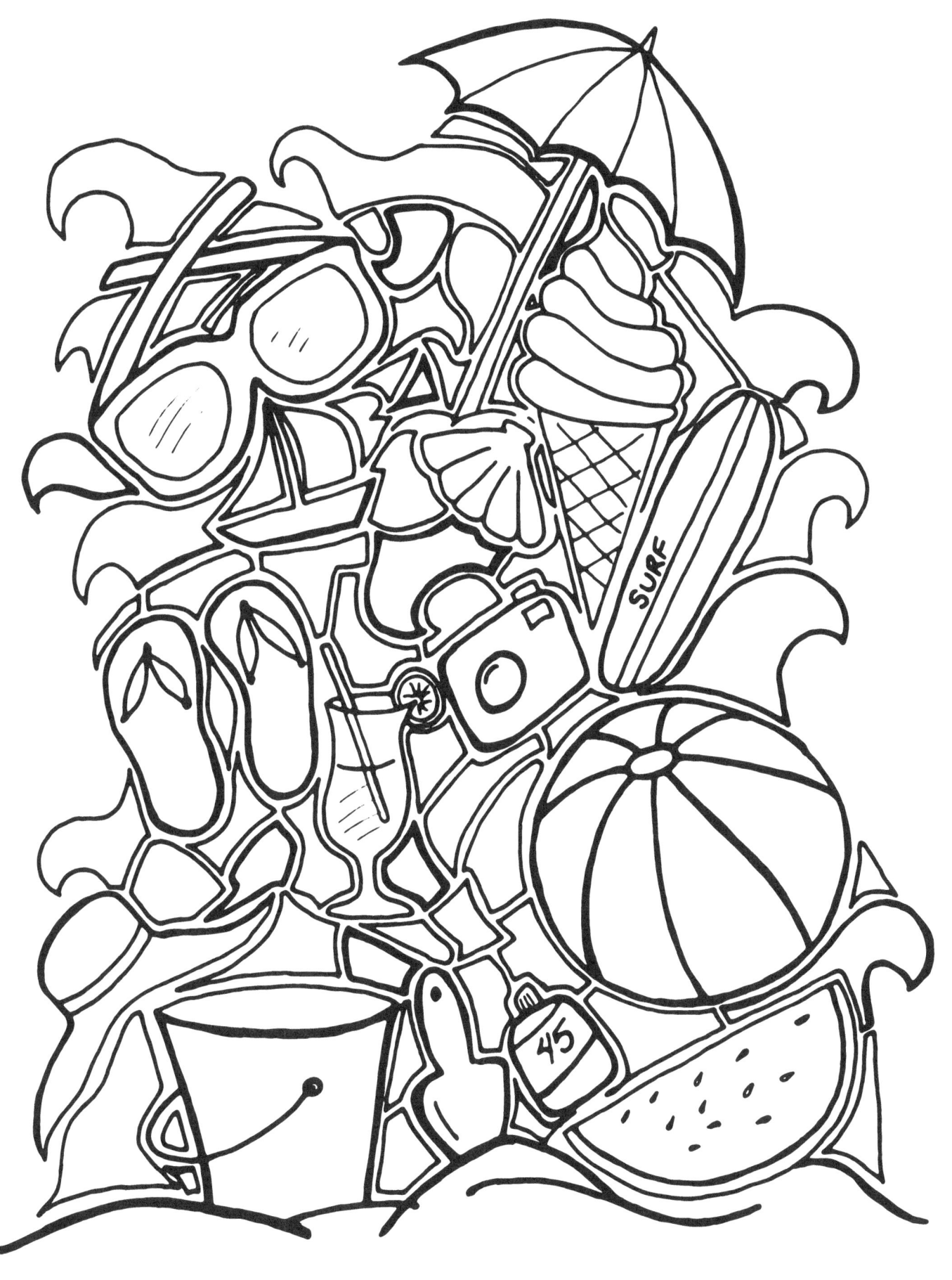

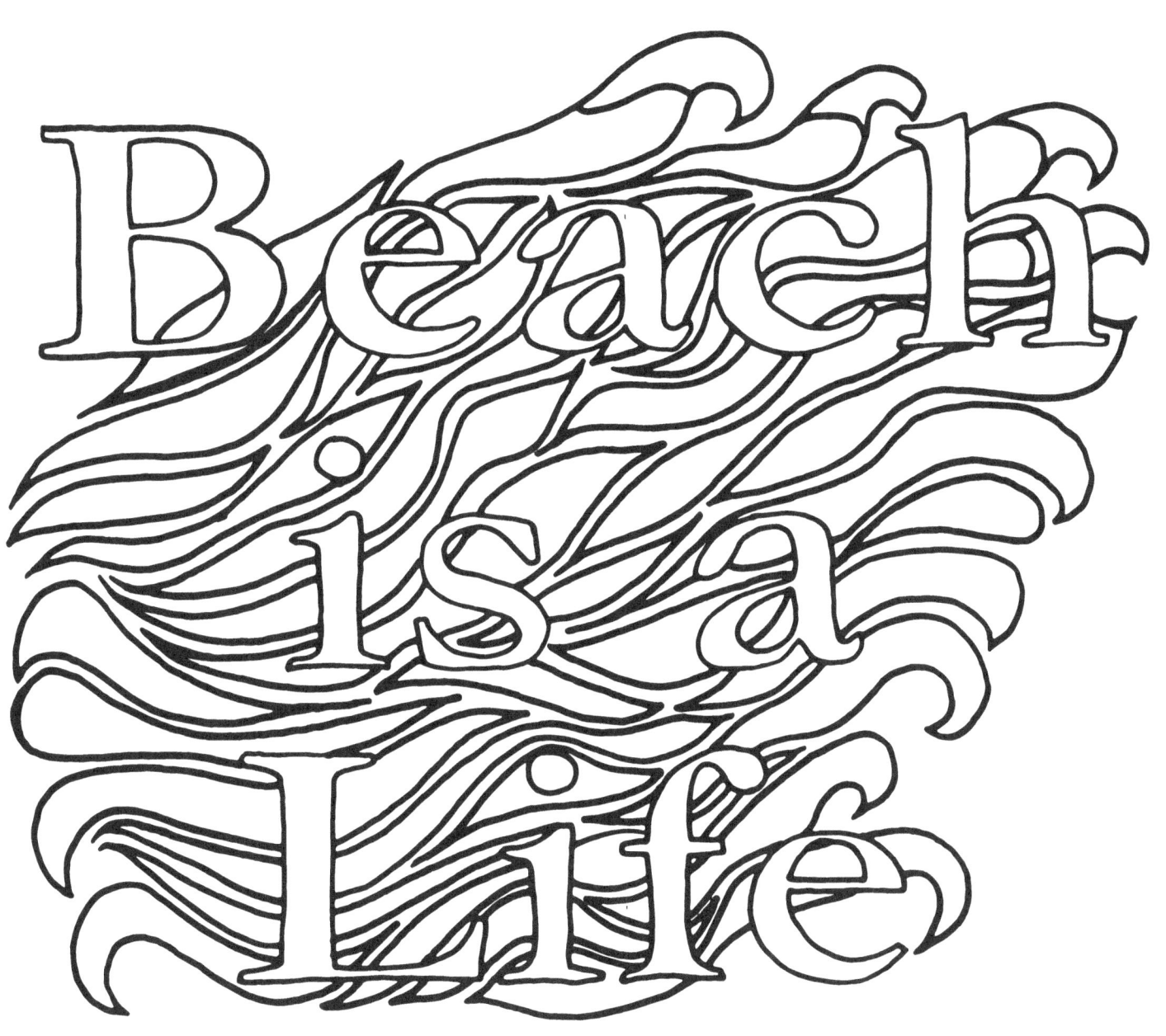

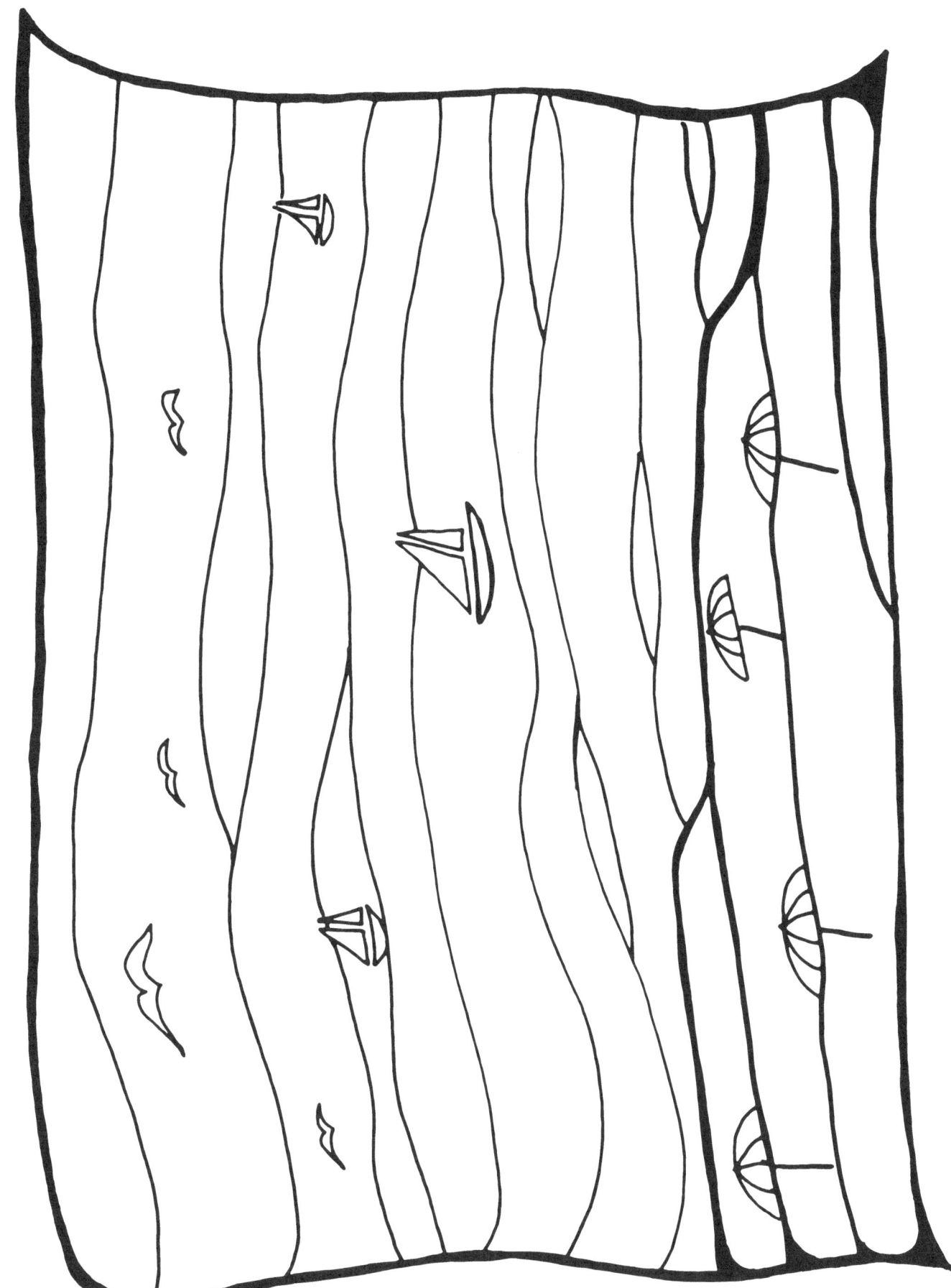

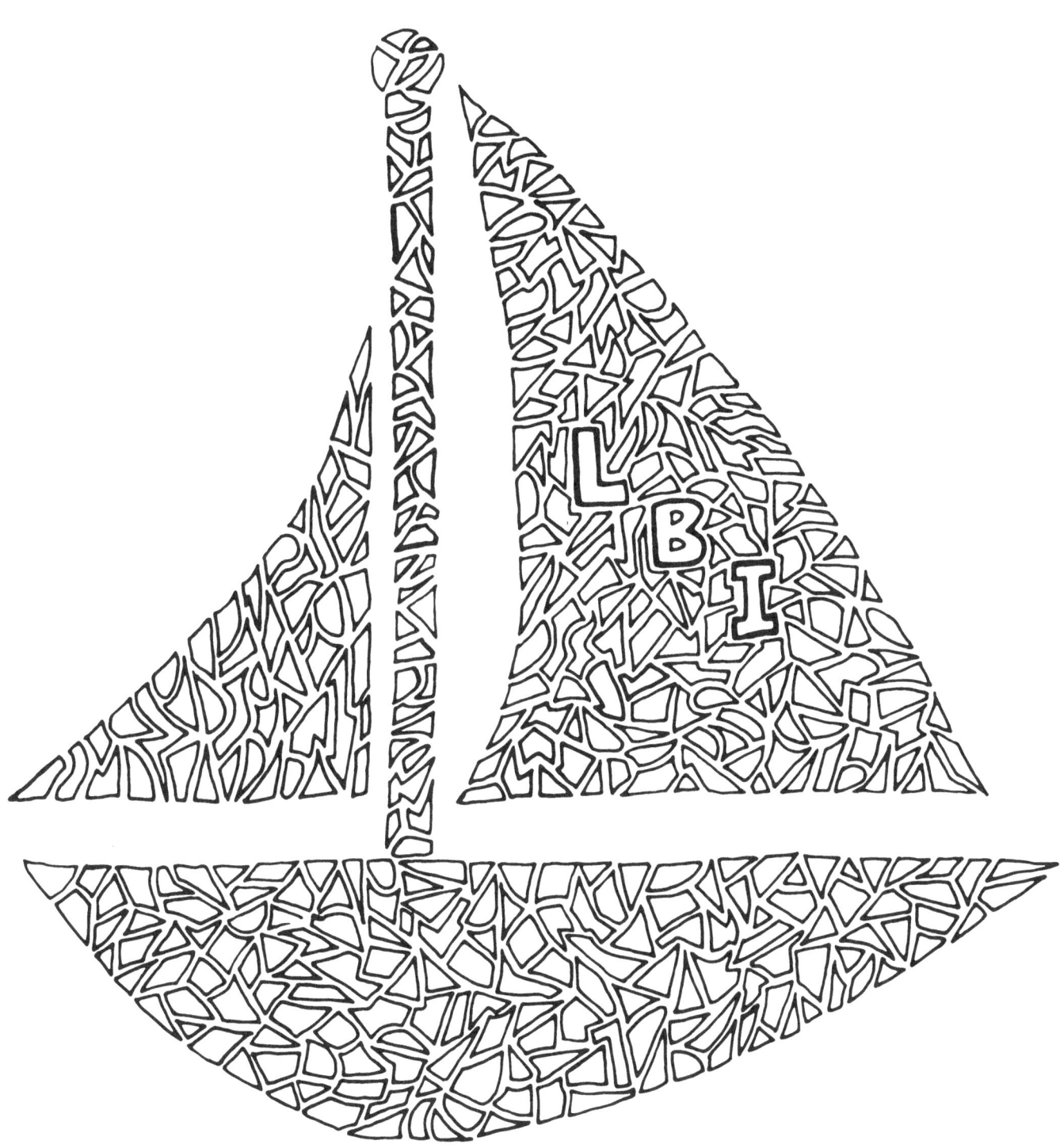

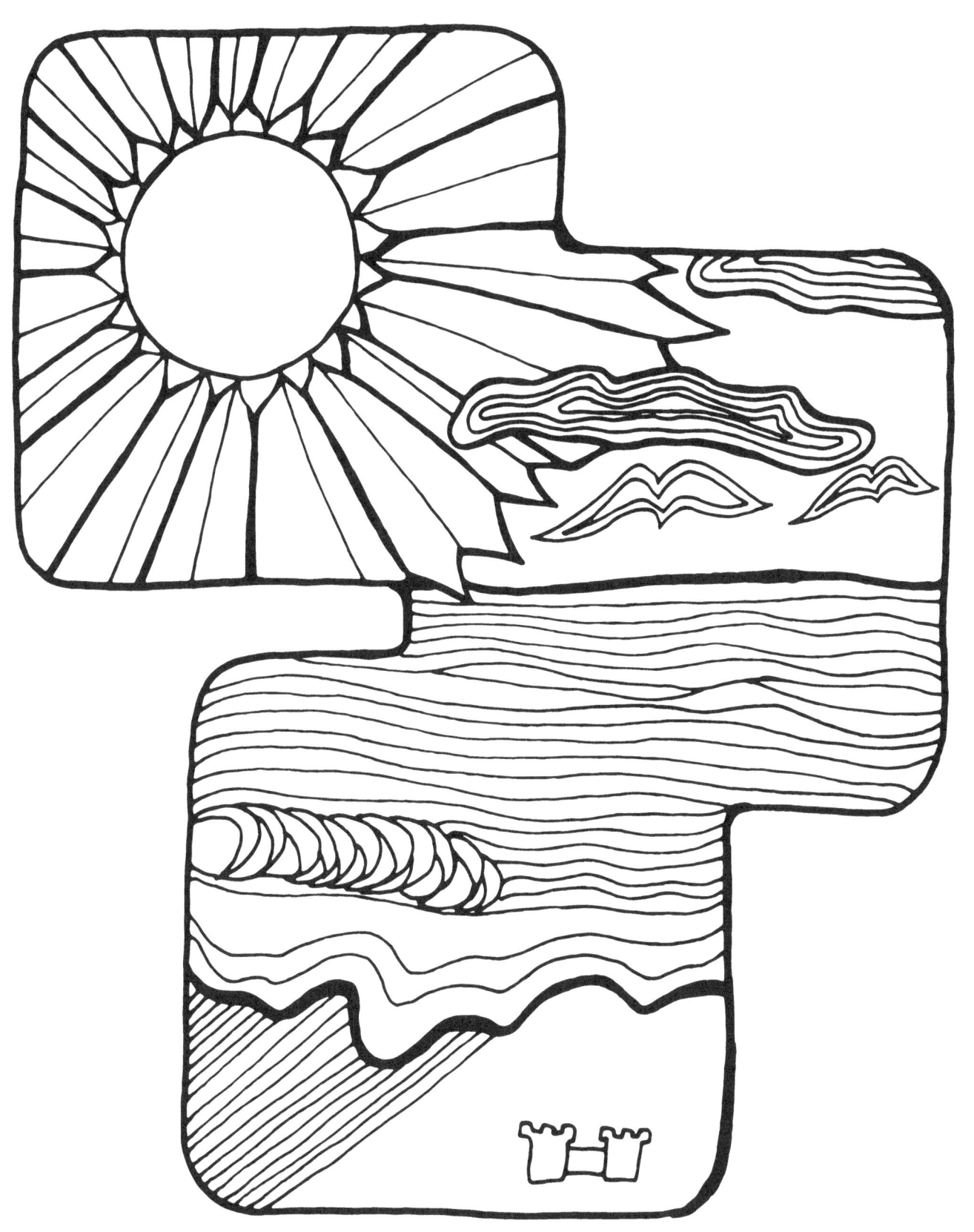

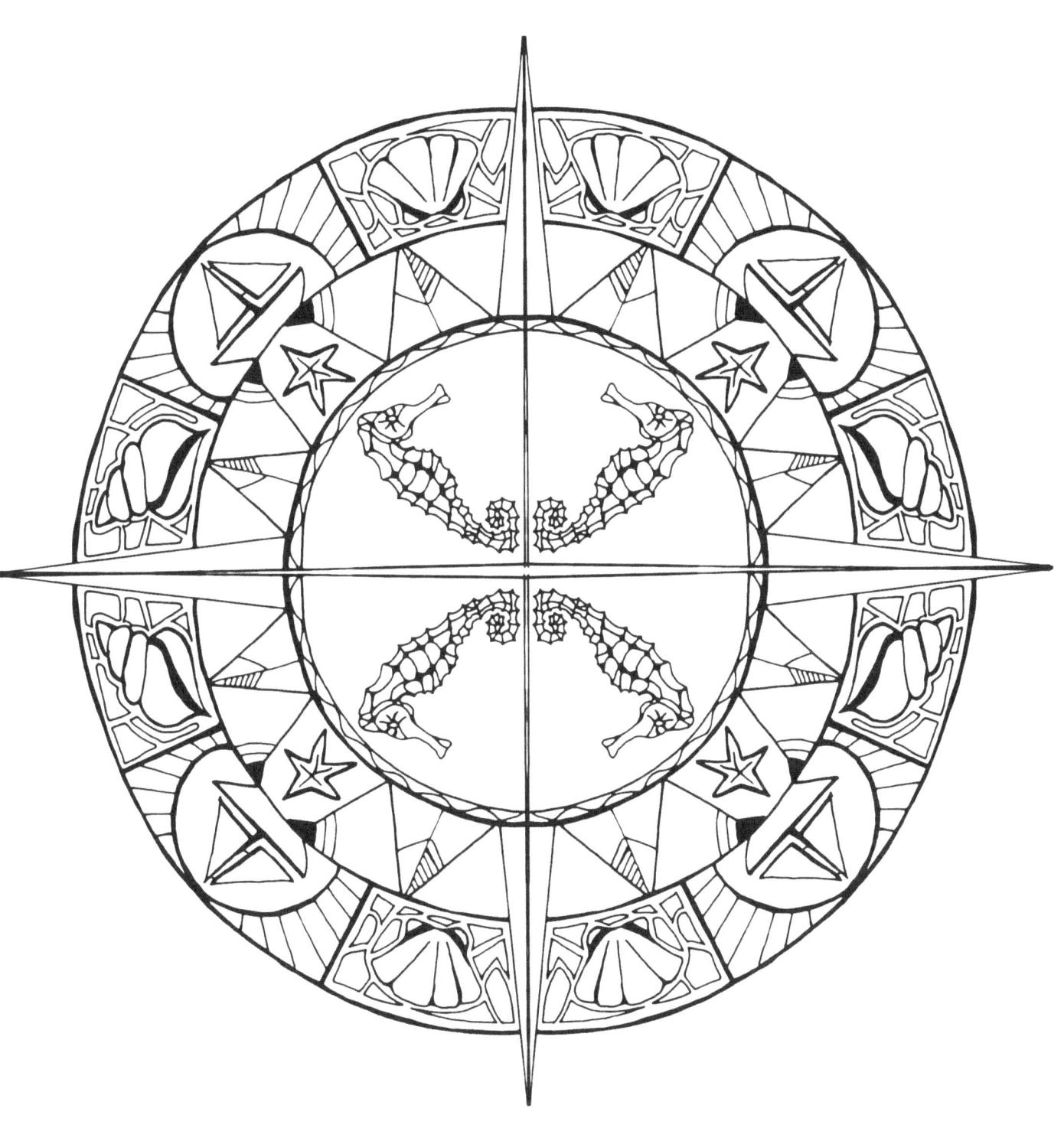

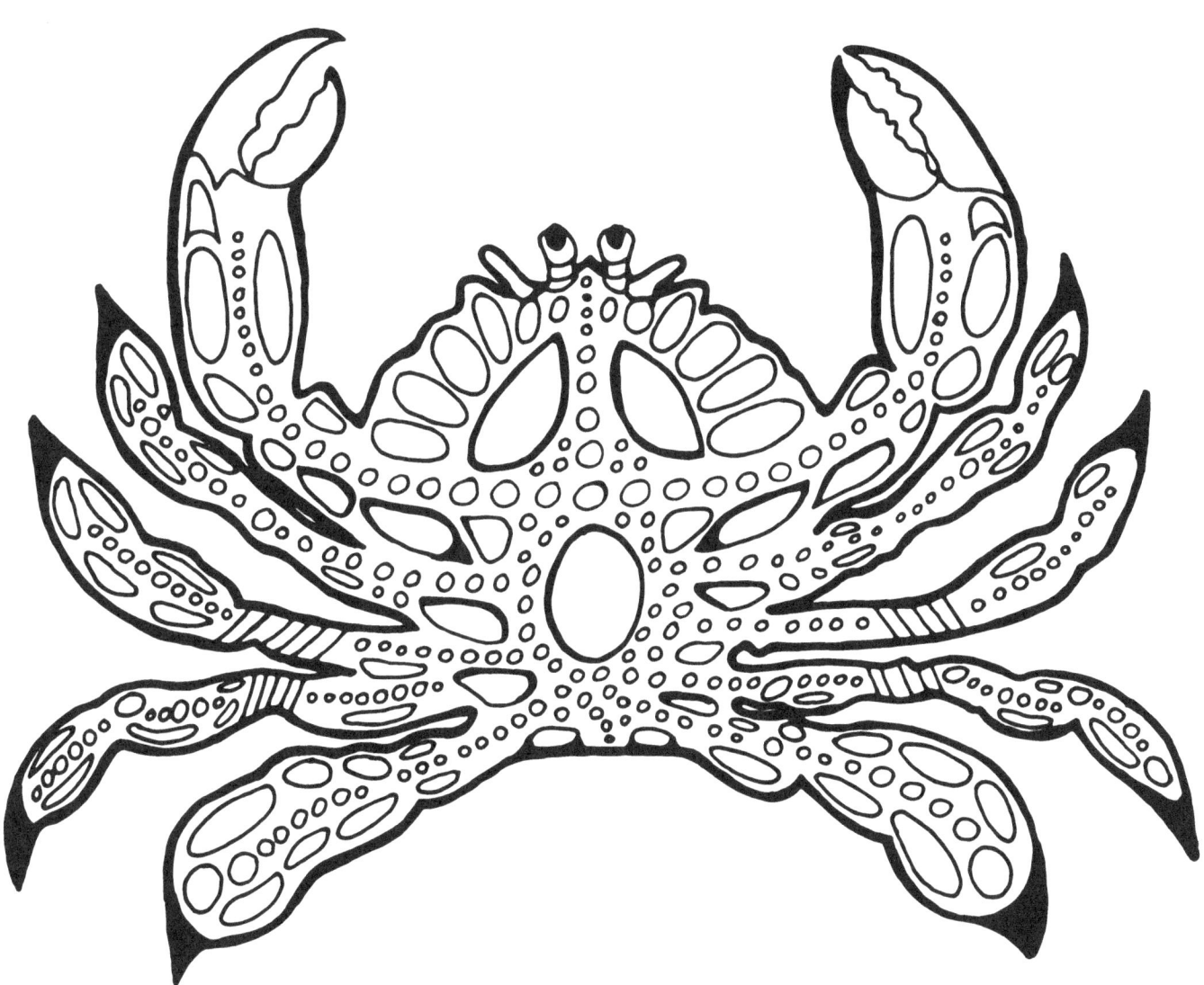

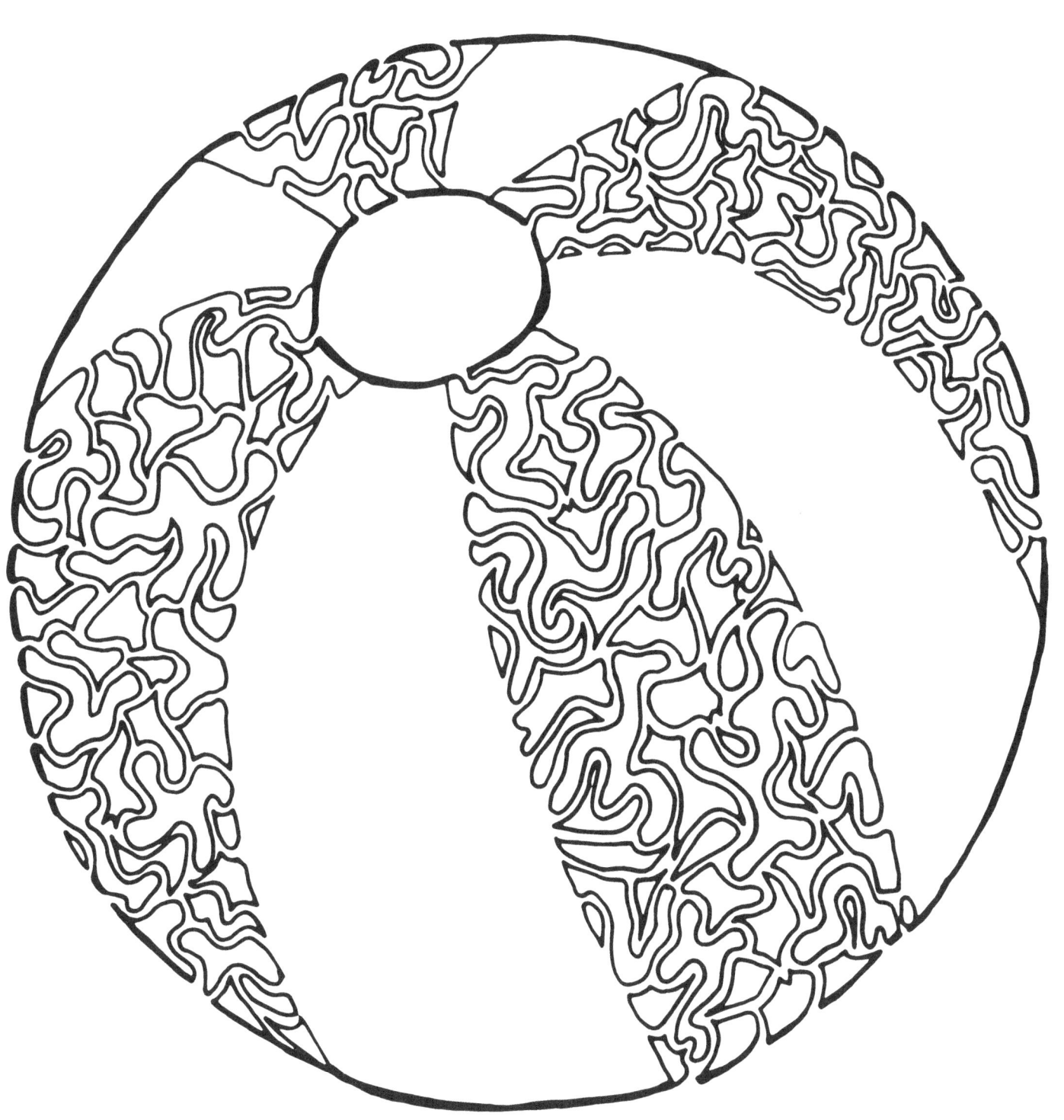

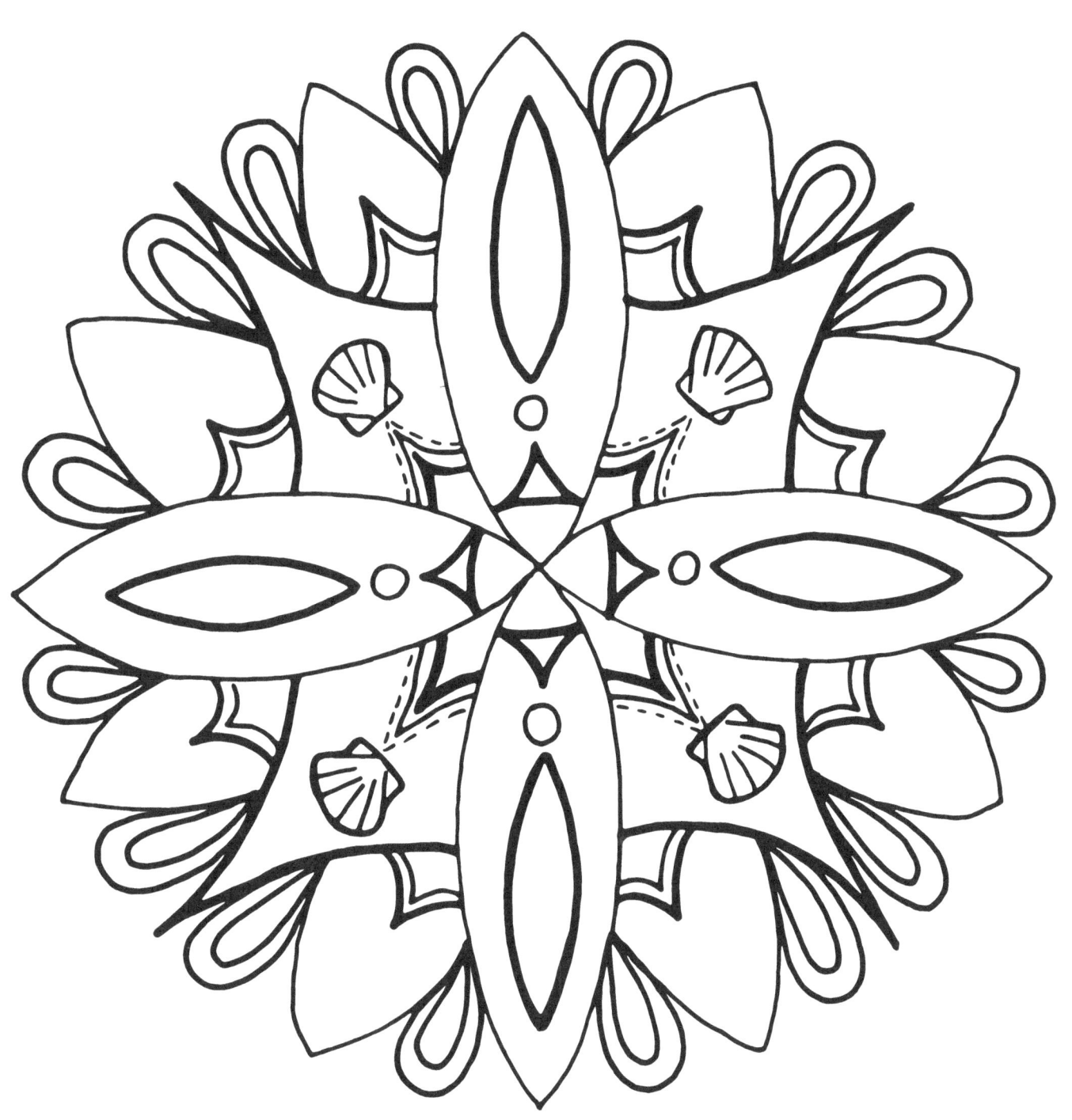

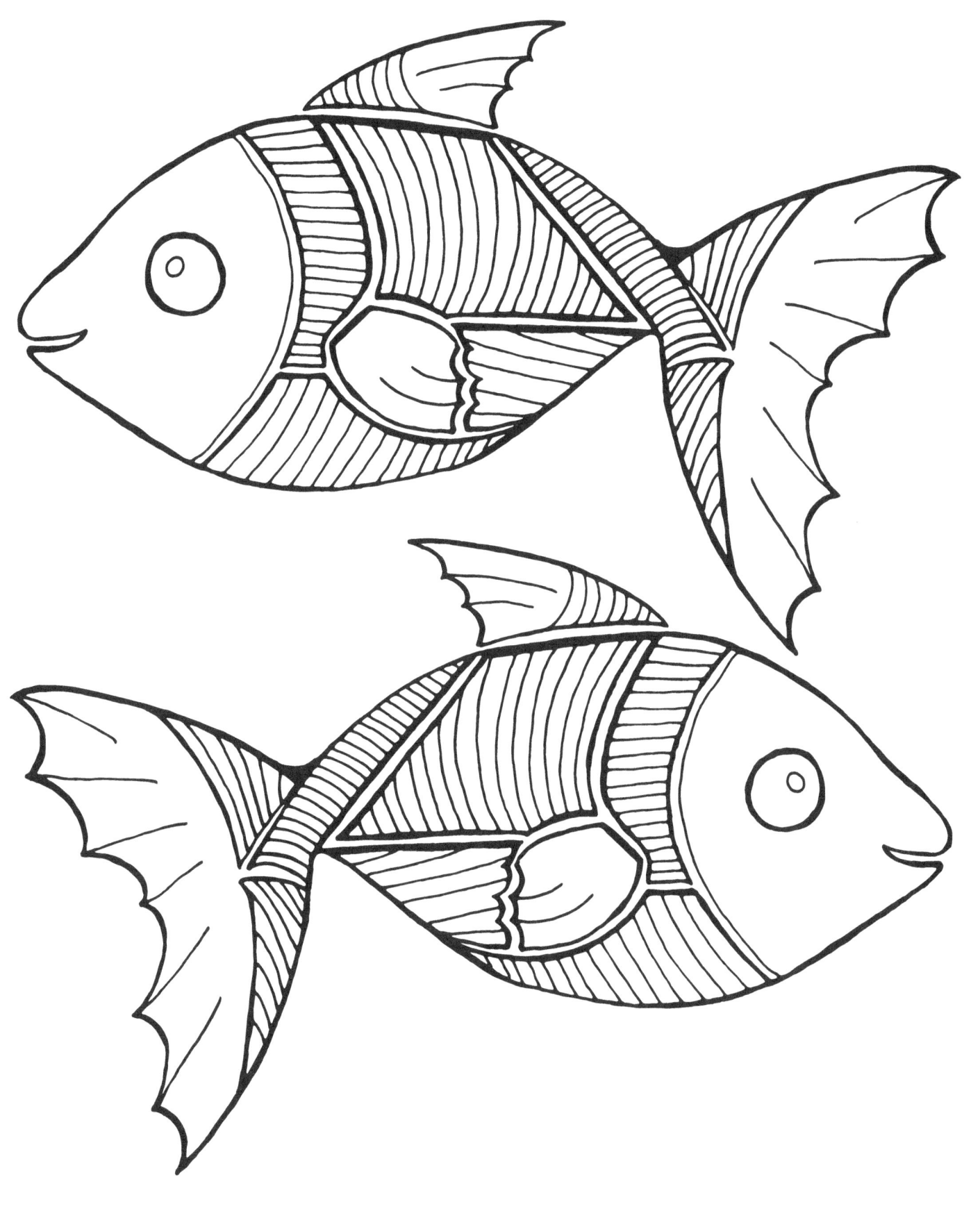

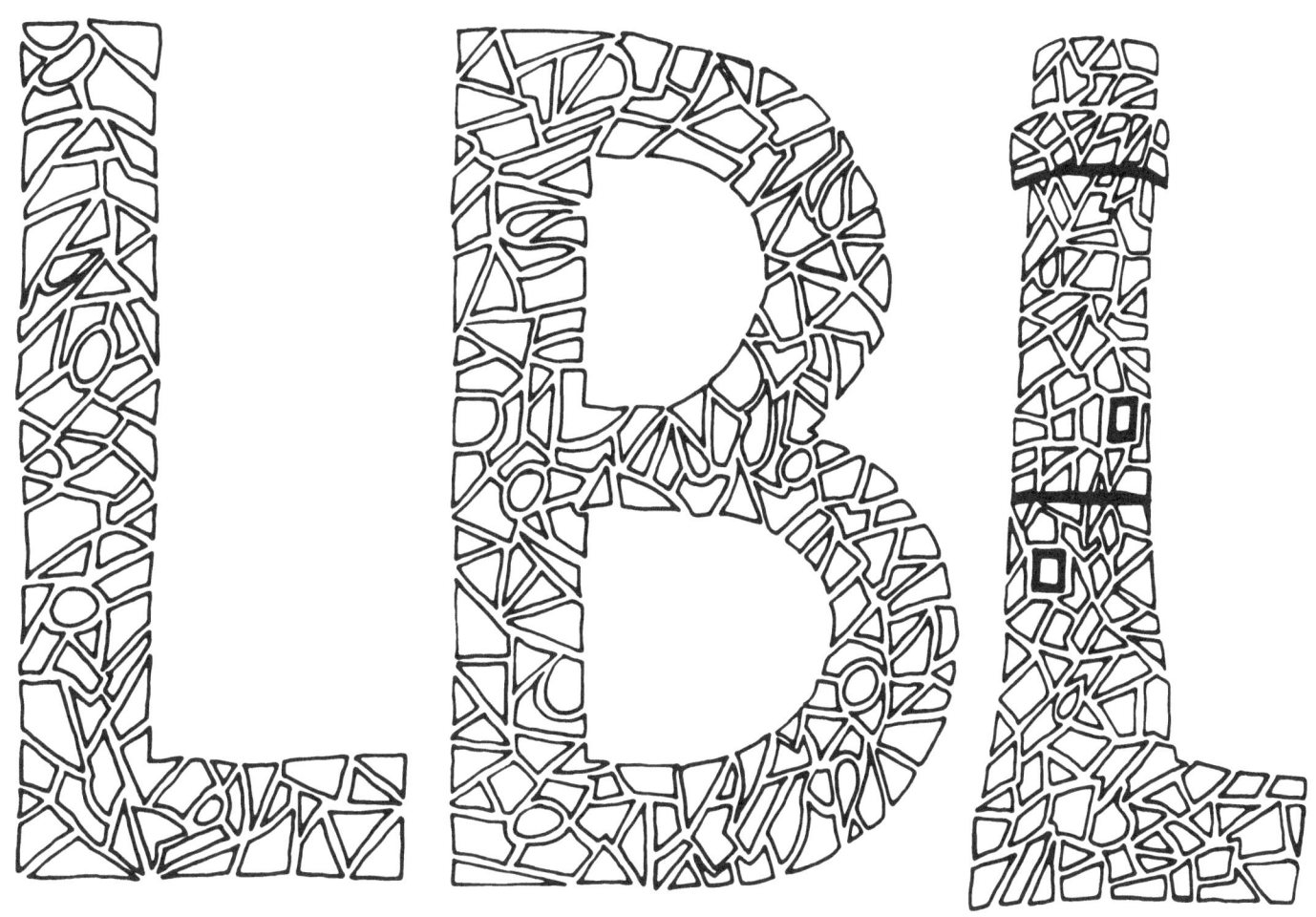

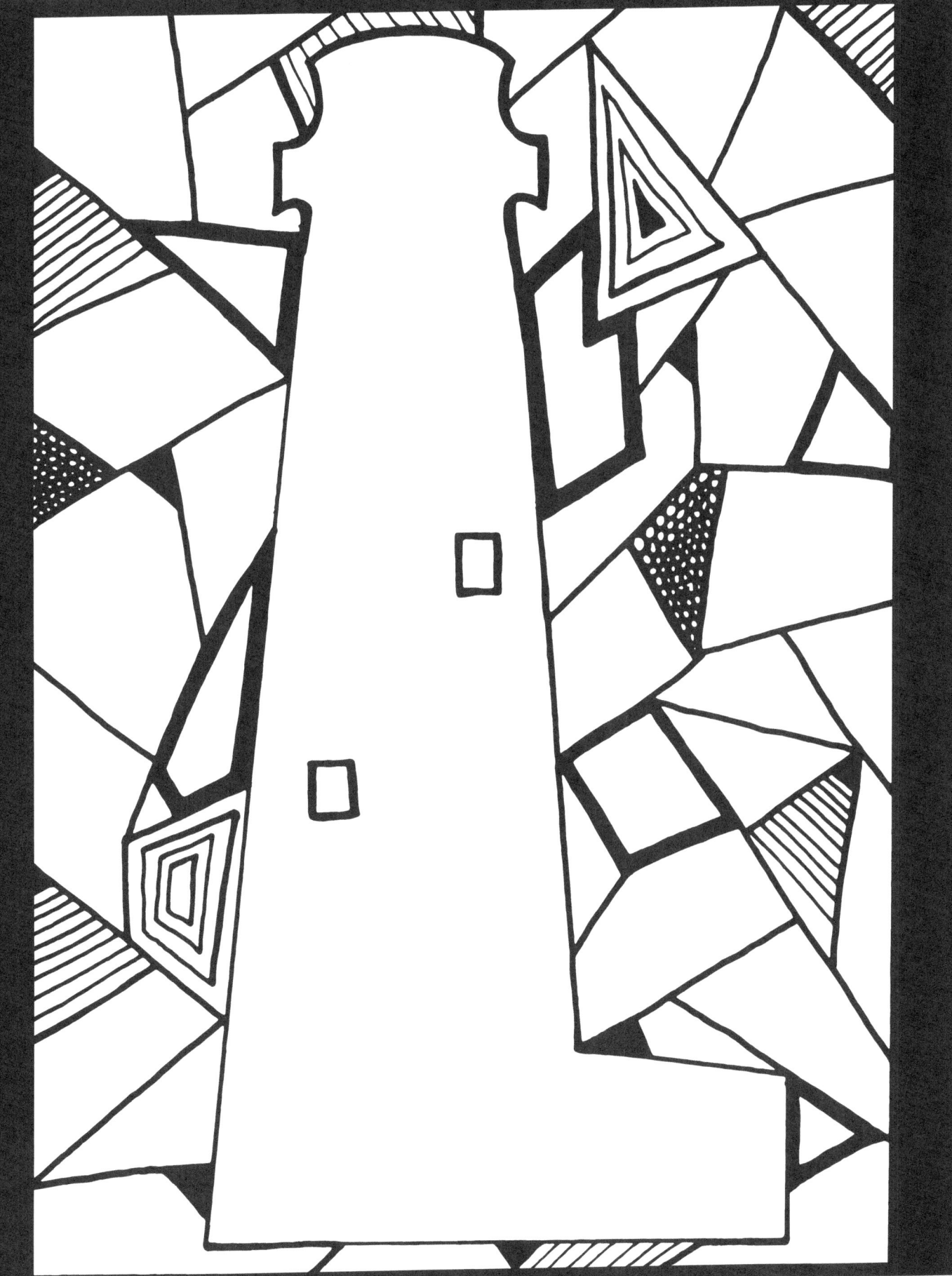

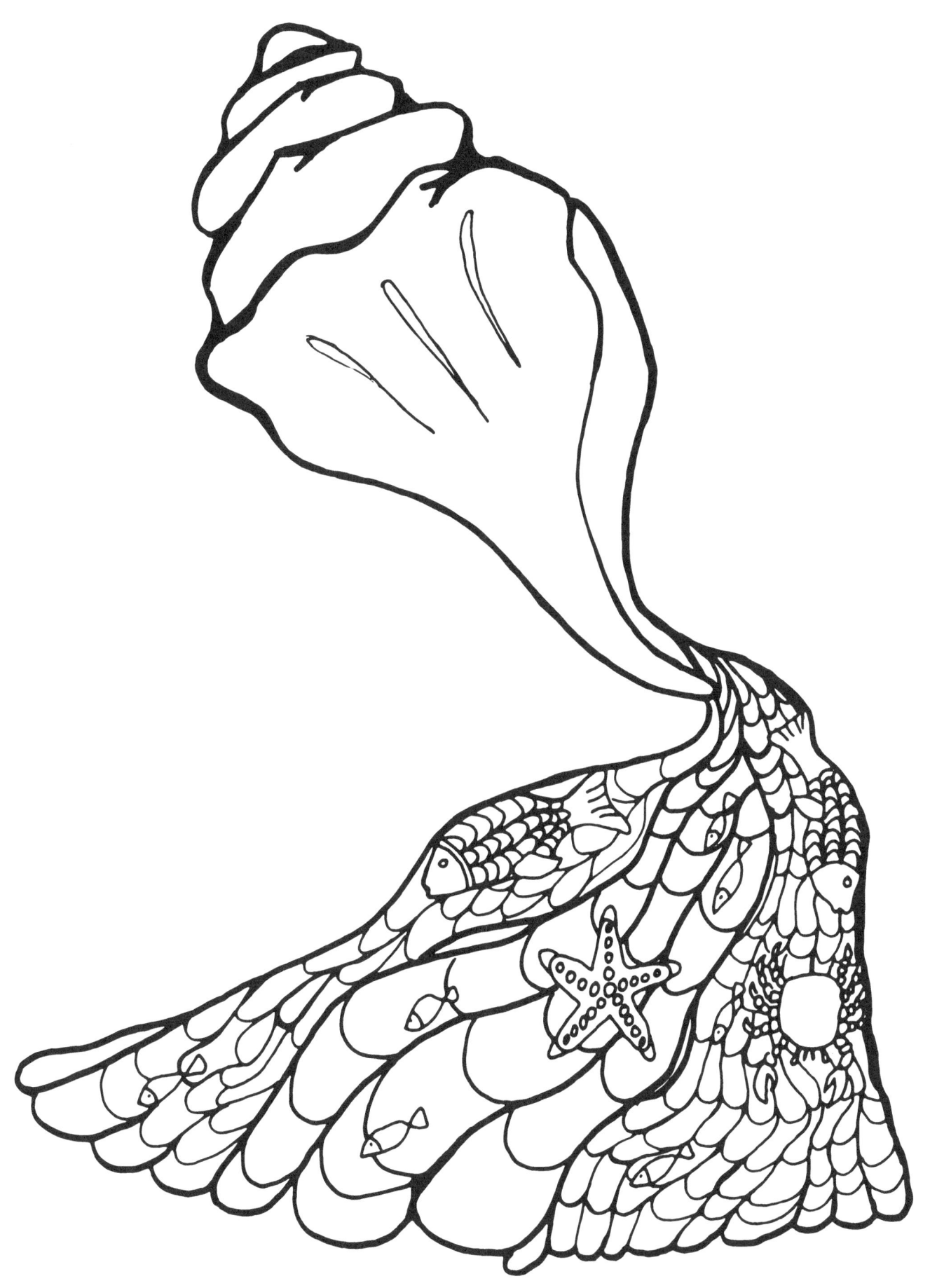

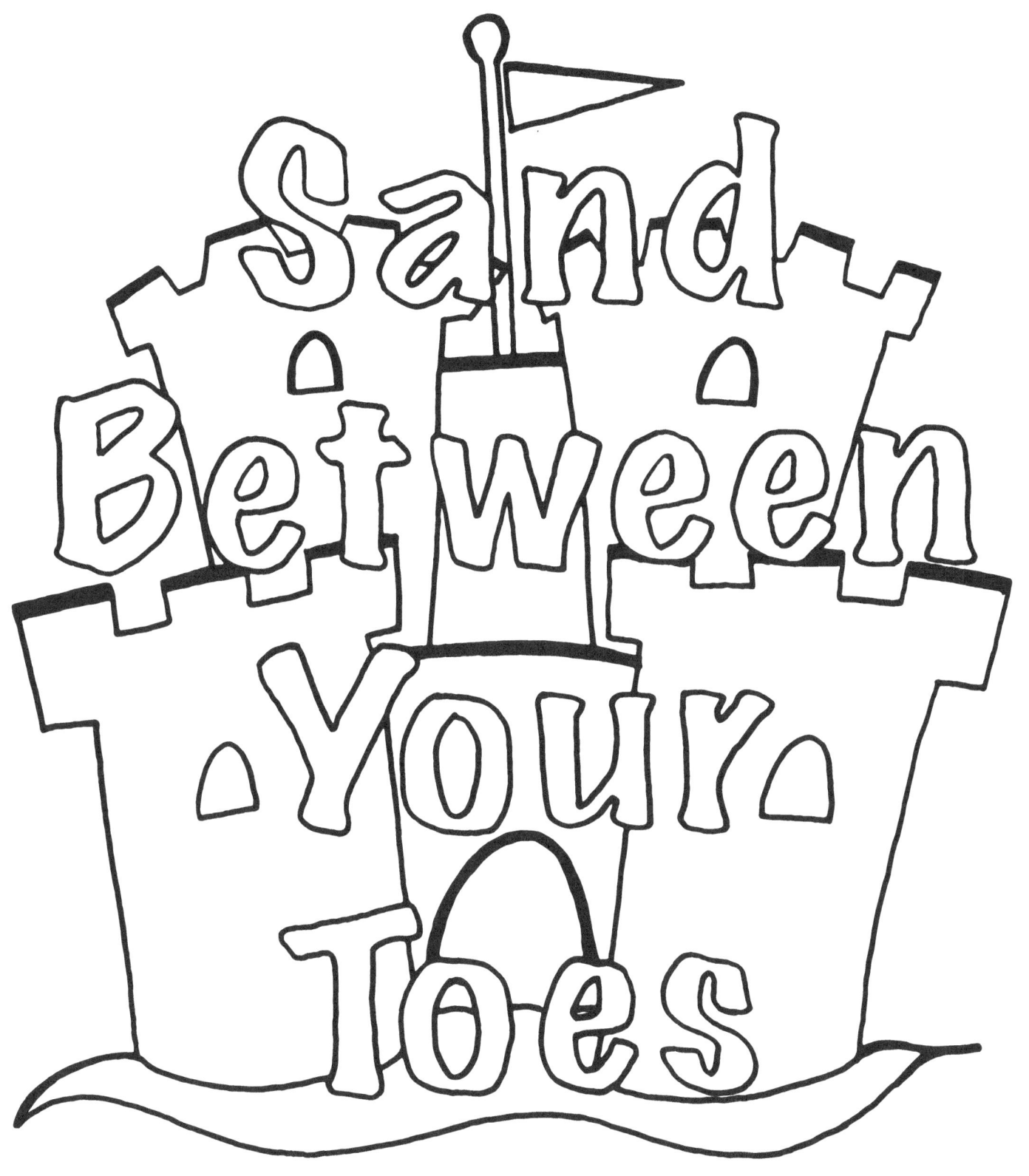

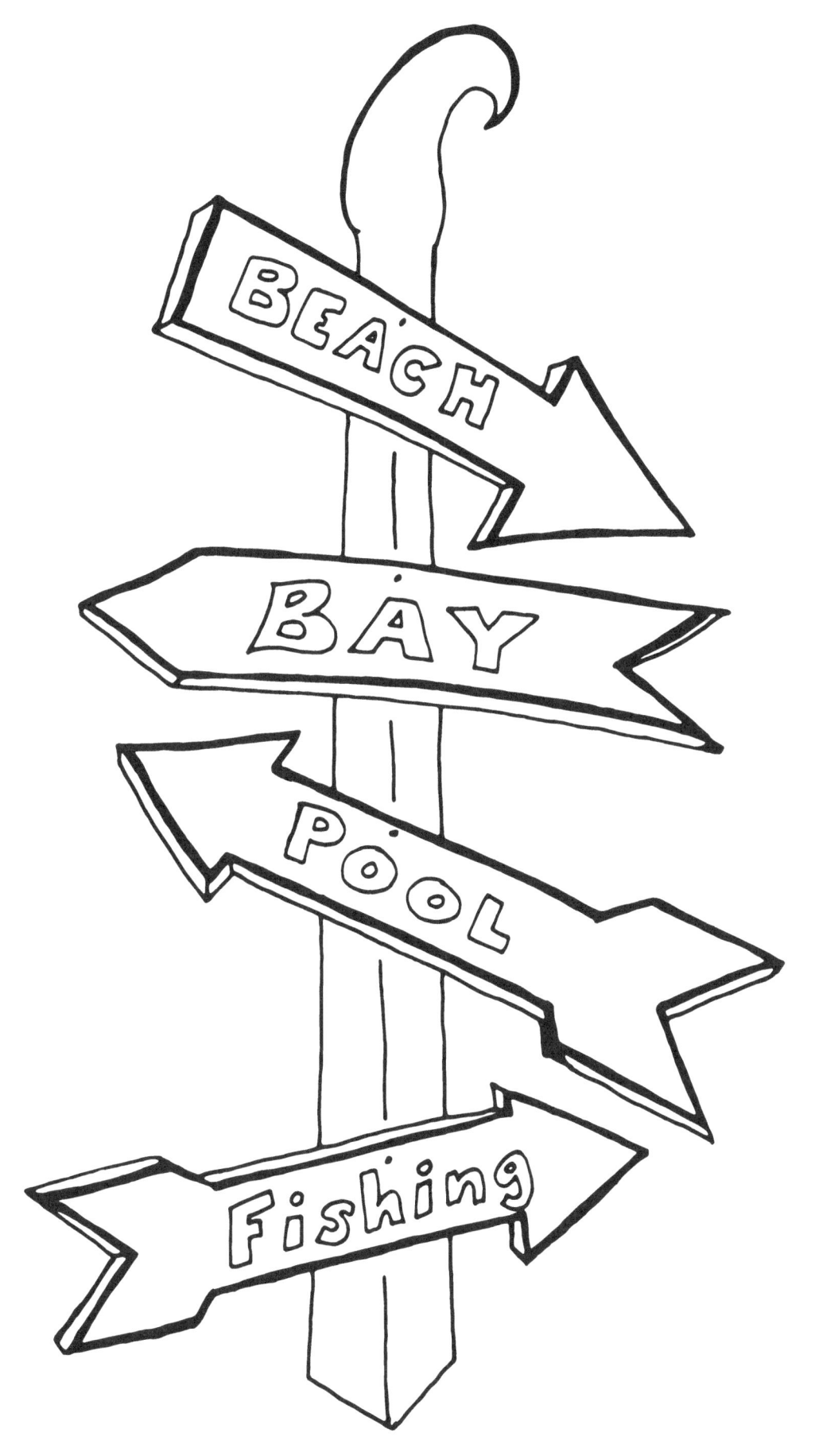

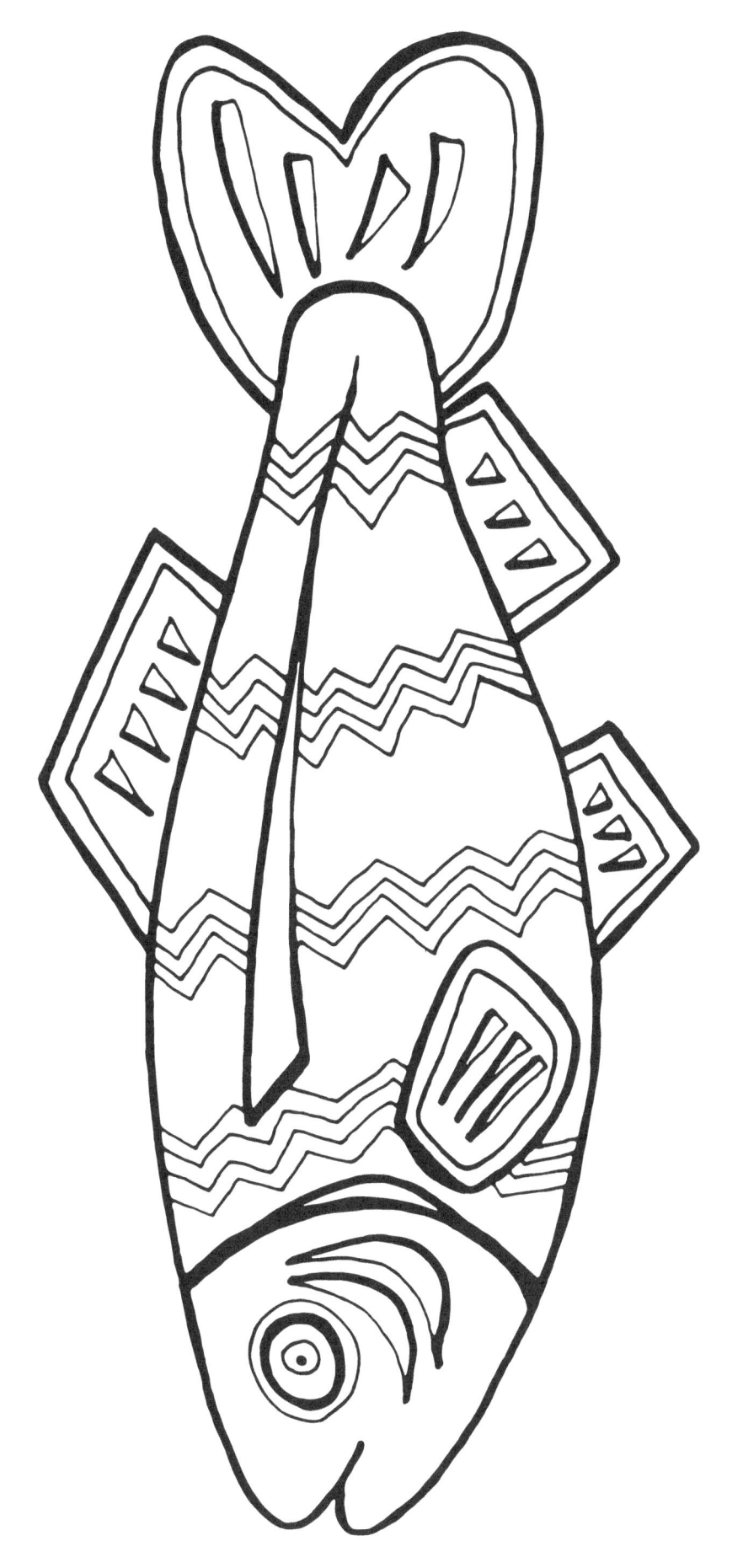

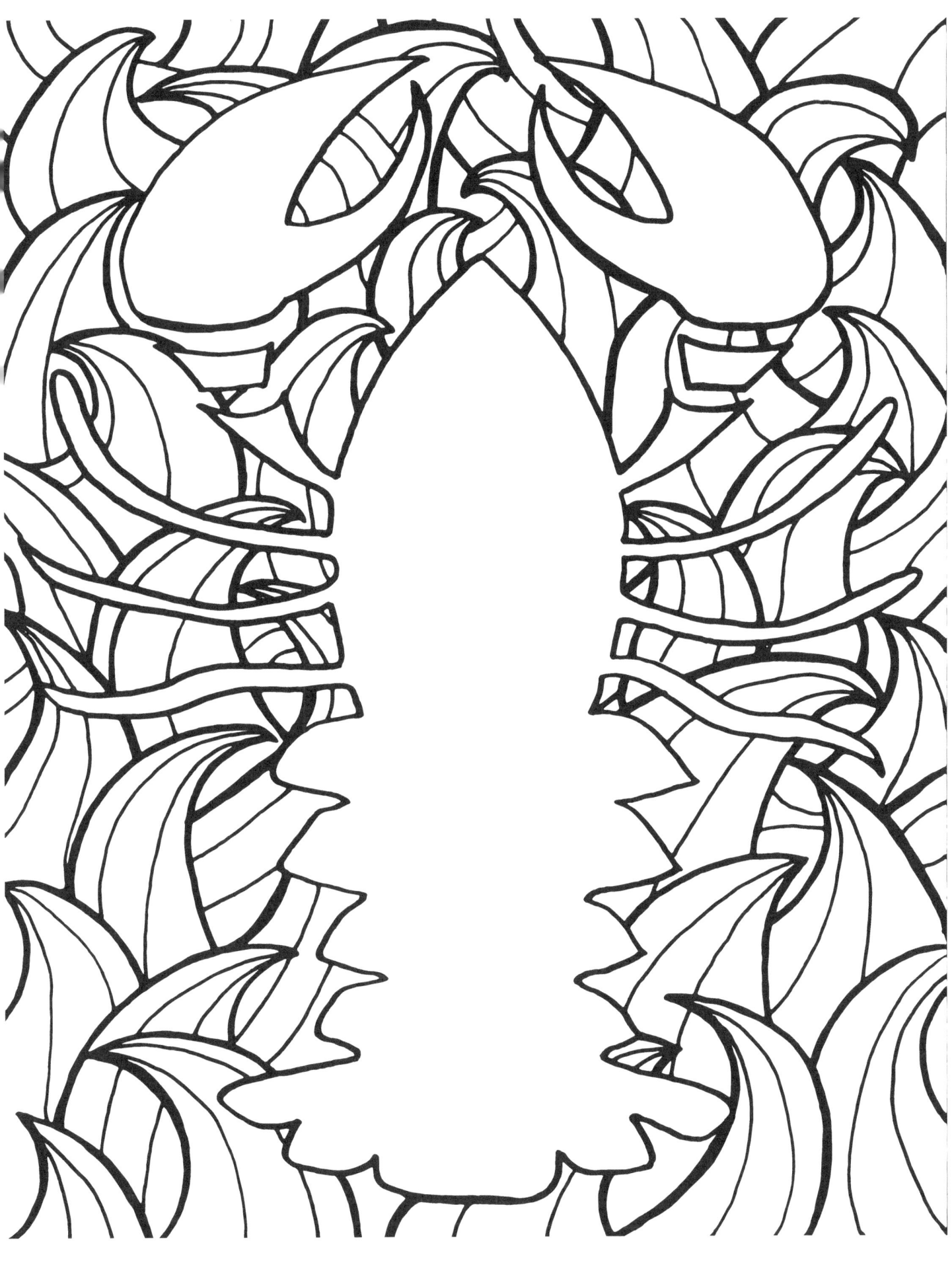

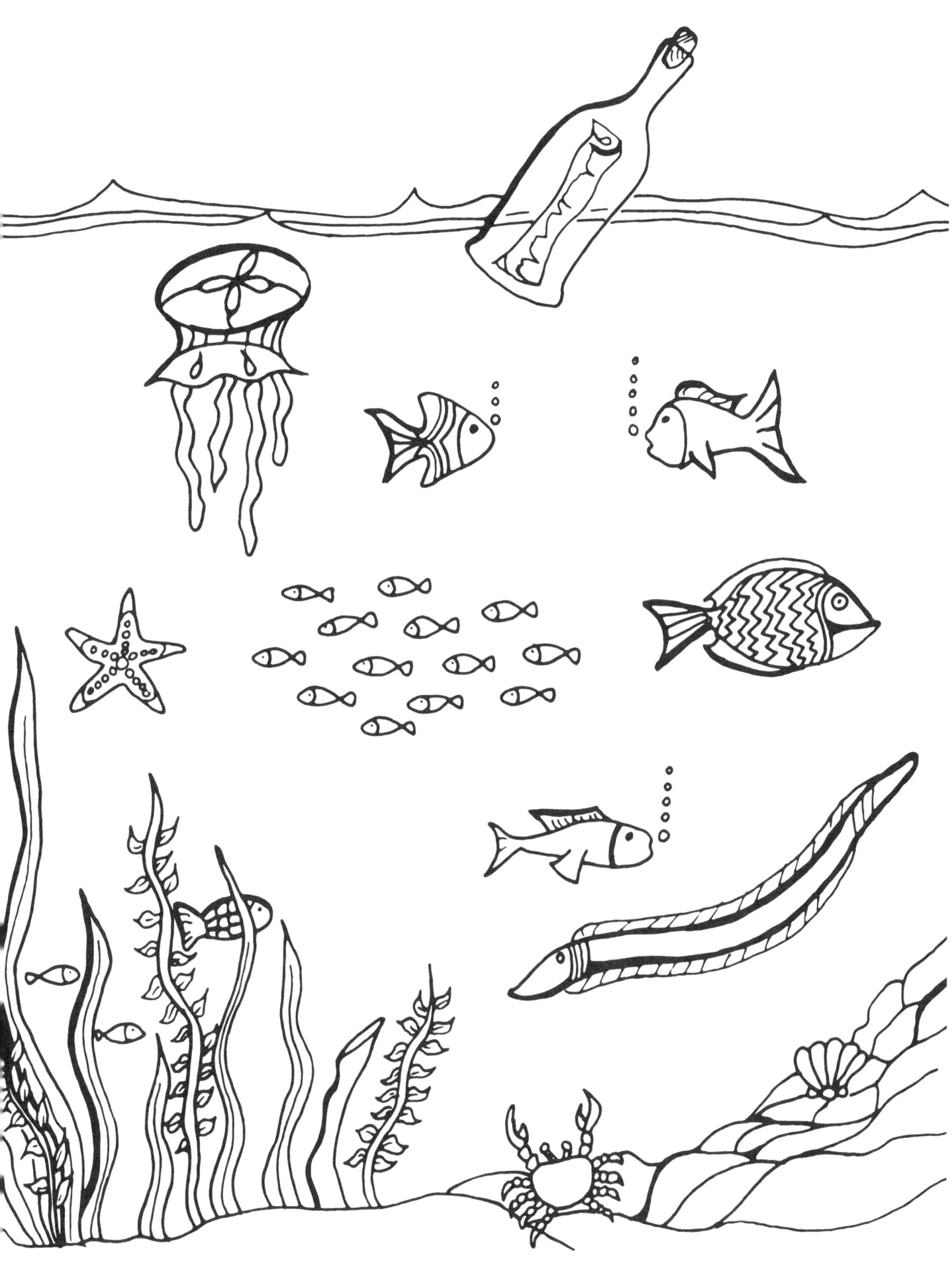

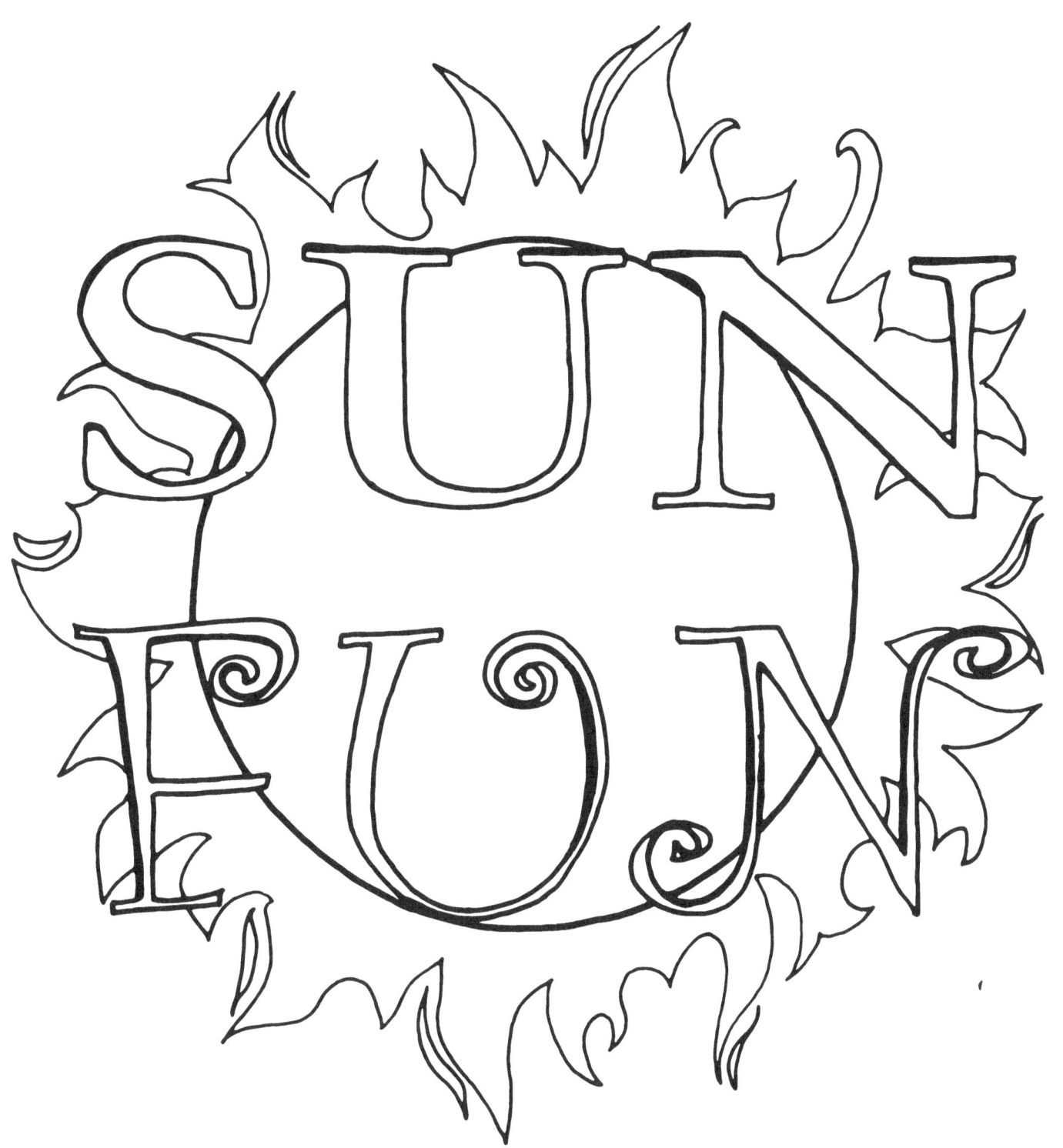

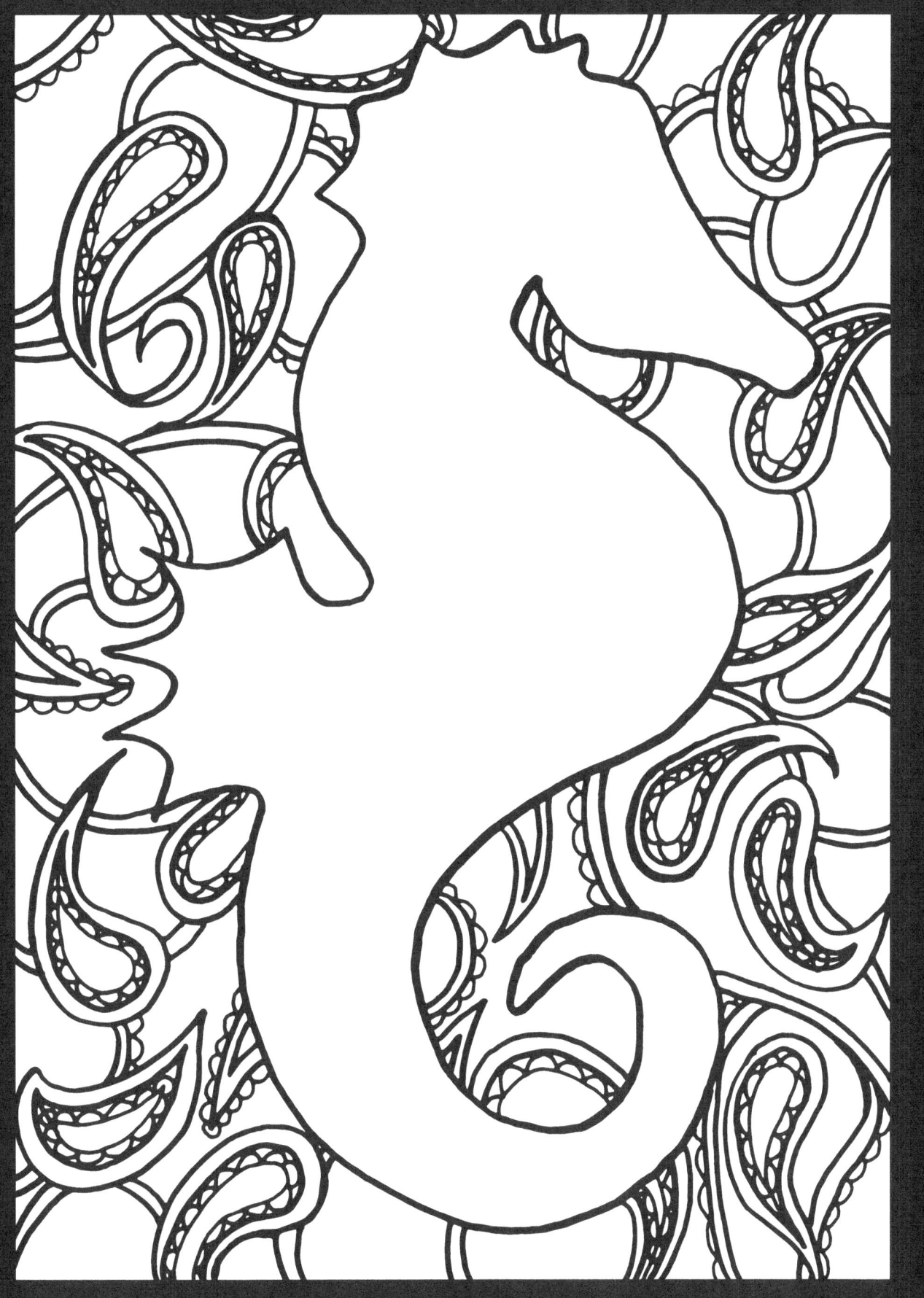

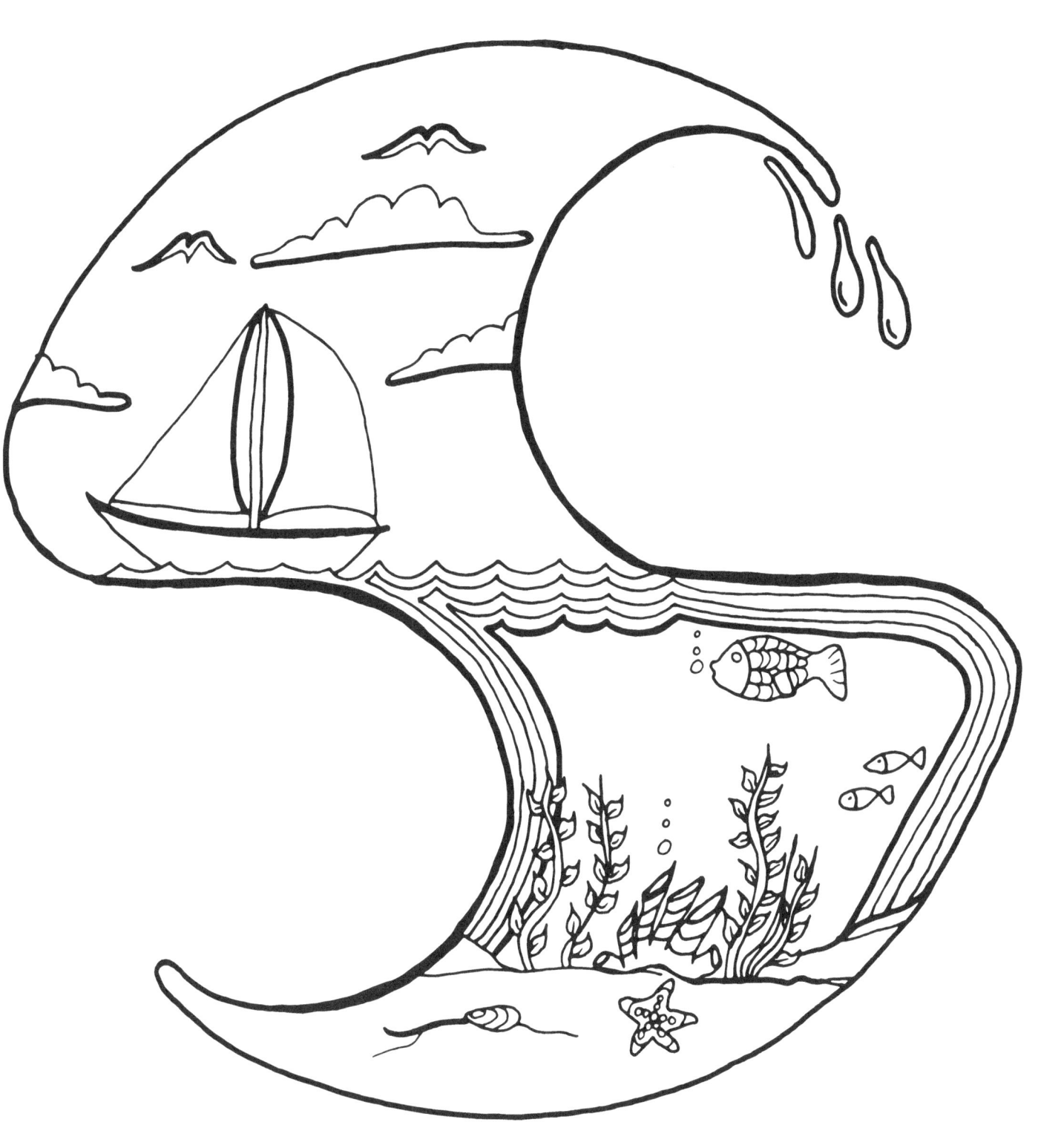

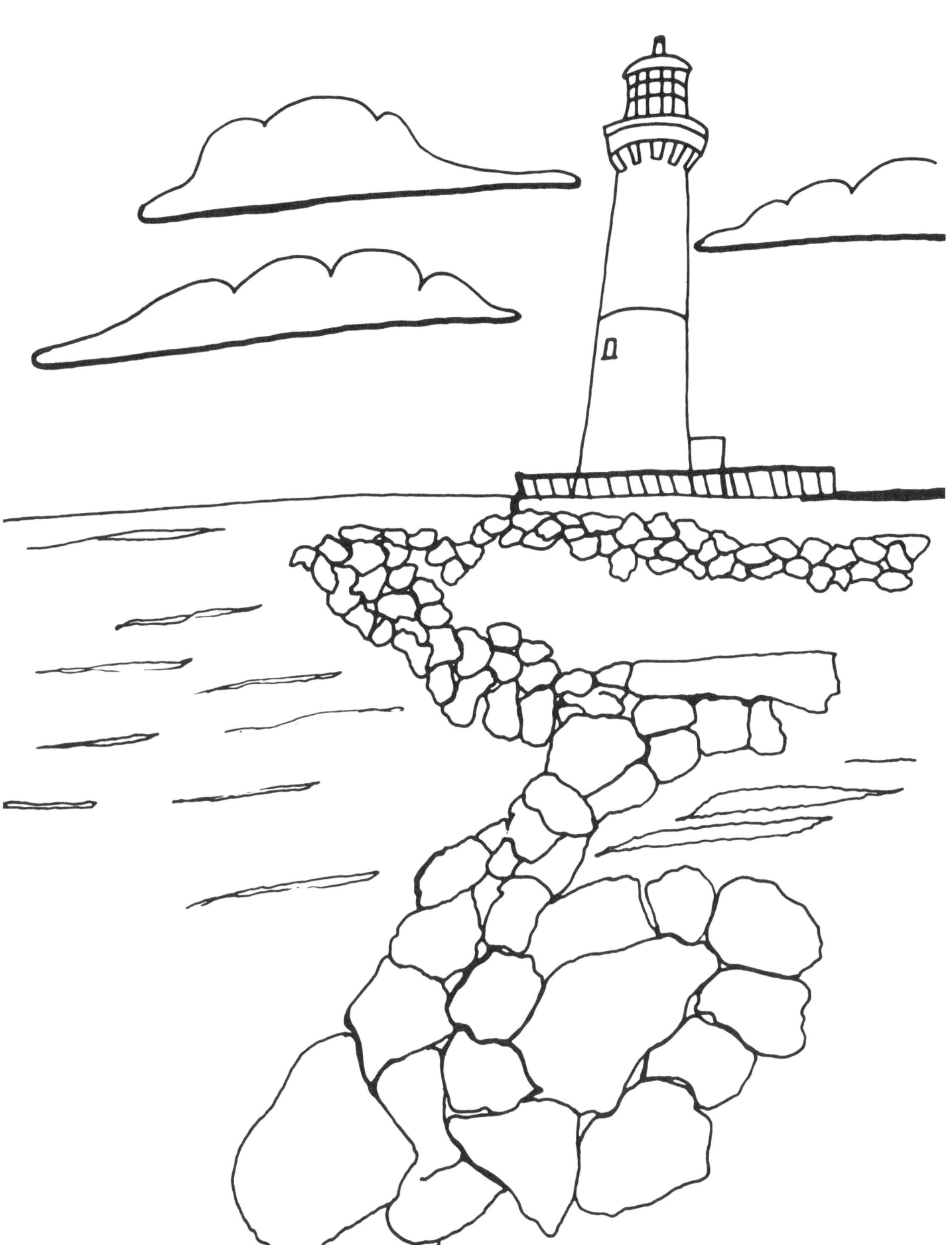

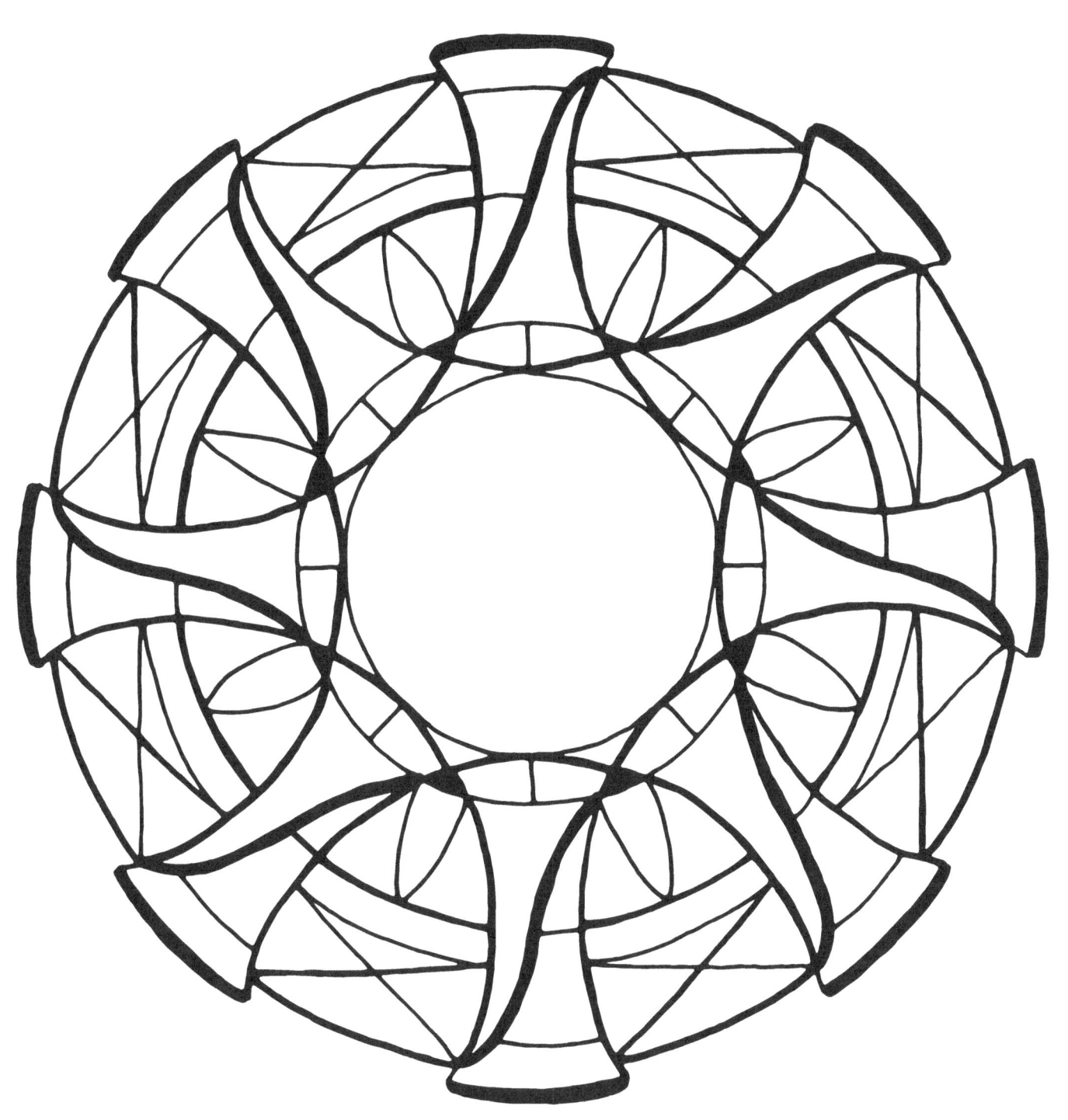

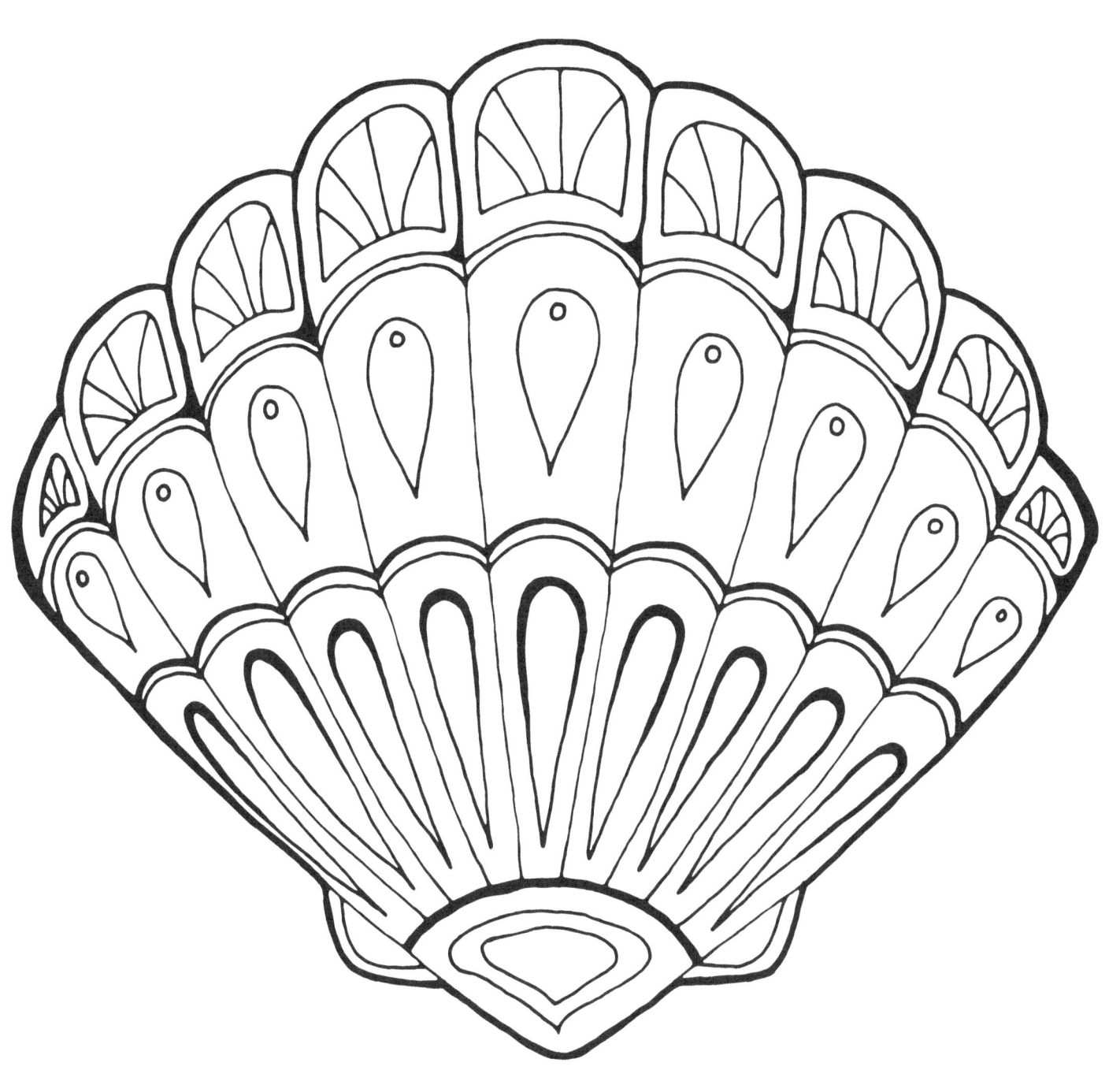

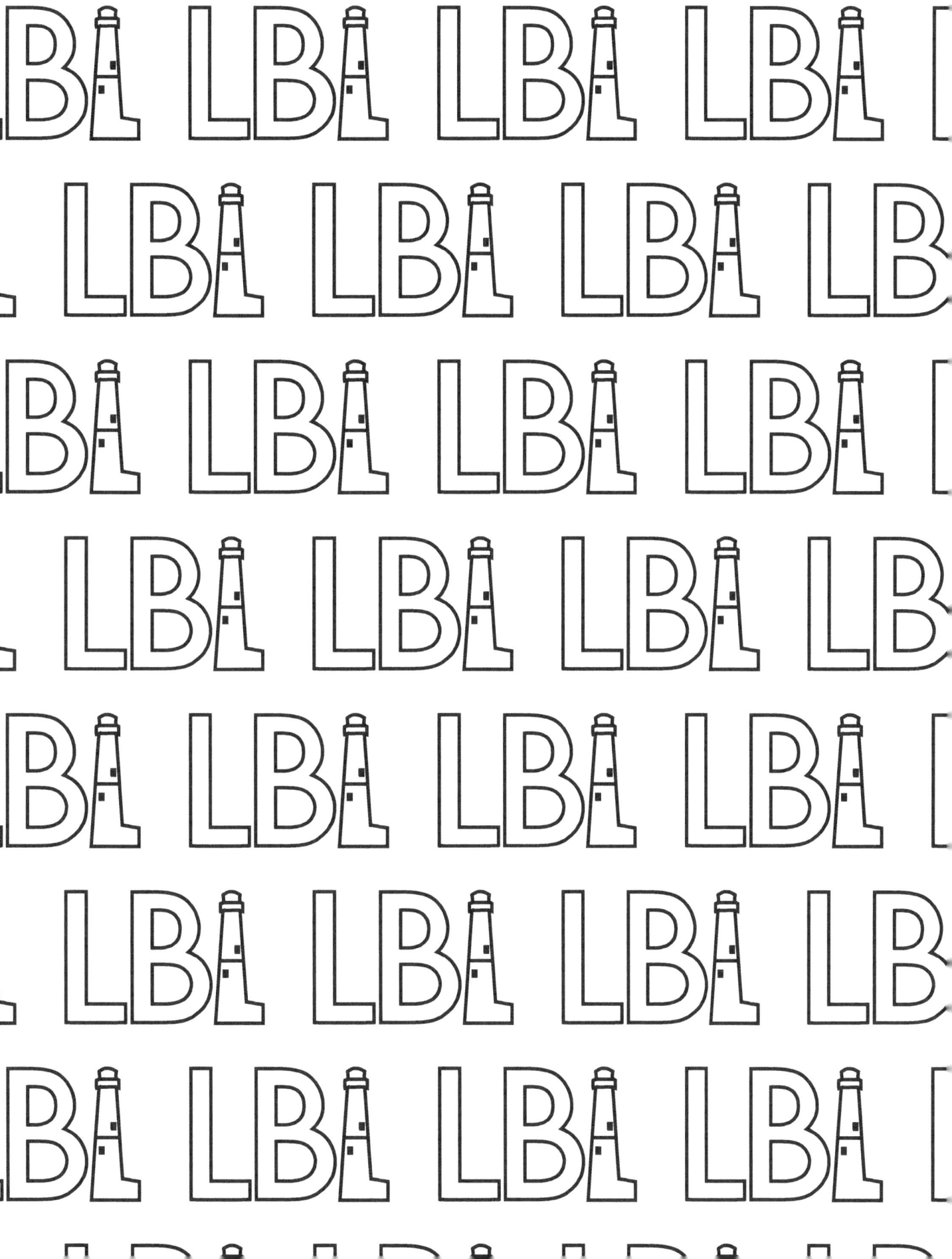

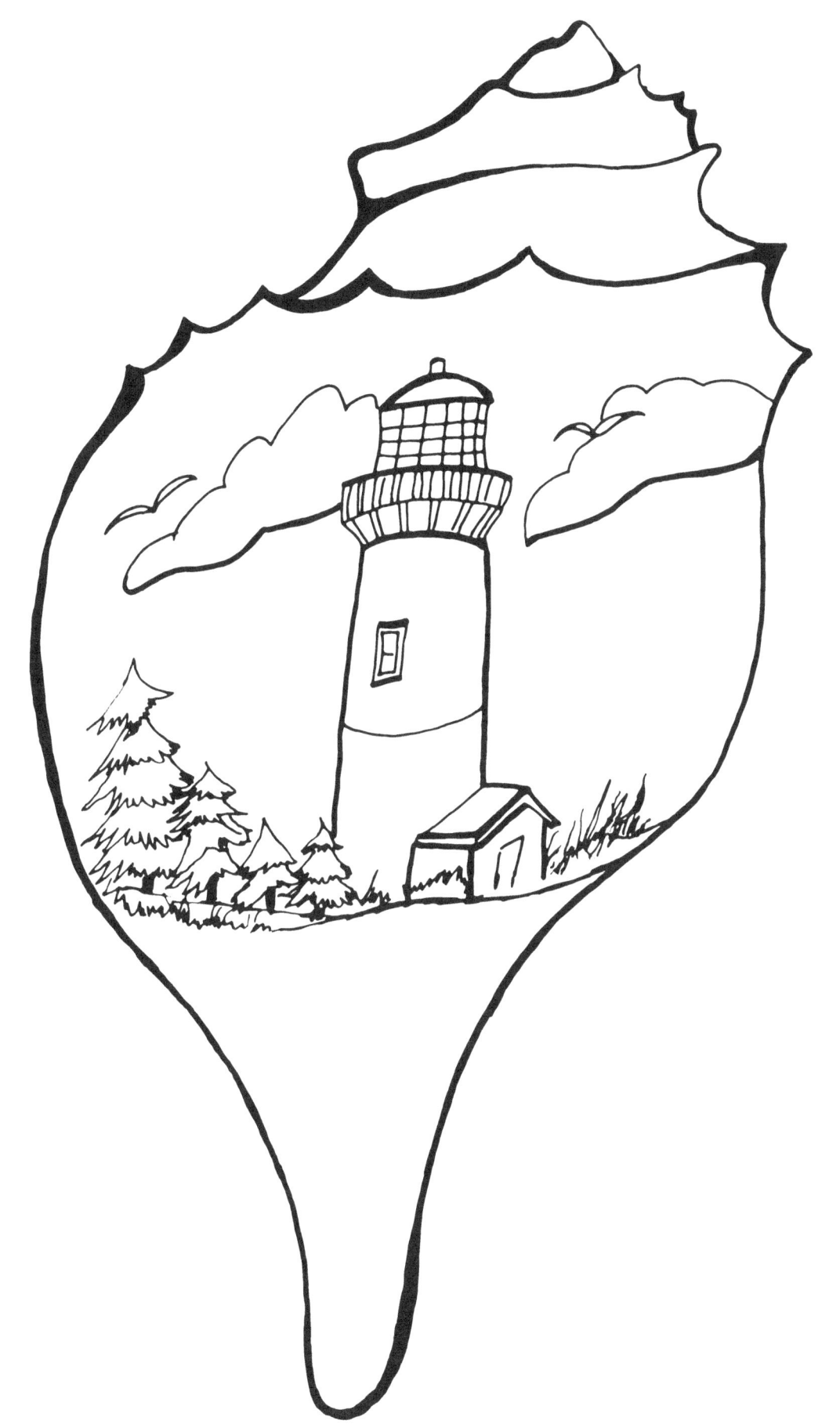

Surf City

Barnegat Light

Spray Beach

Beach Haven

Brant Beach

Peahala Park Brighton Beach

Beach Haven Crest Haven Beach

Harvey Cedars

Beach Haven Gardens Beach Haven Terrace

Long Beach Township

Holgate

SHIP BOTTOM Loveladies

Beach Haven Park Beach Haven Inlet

High Bar Harbor

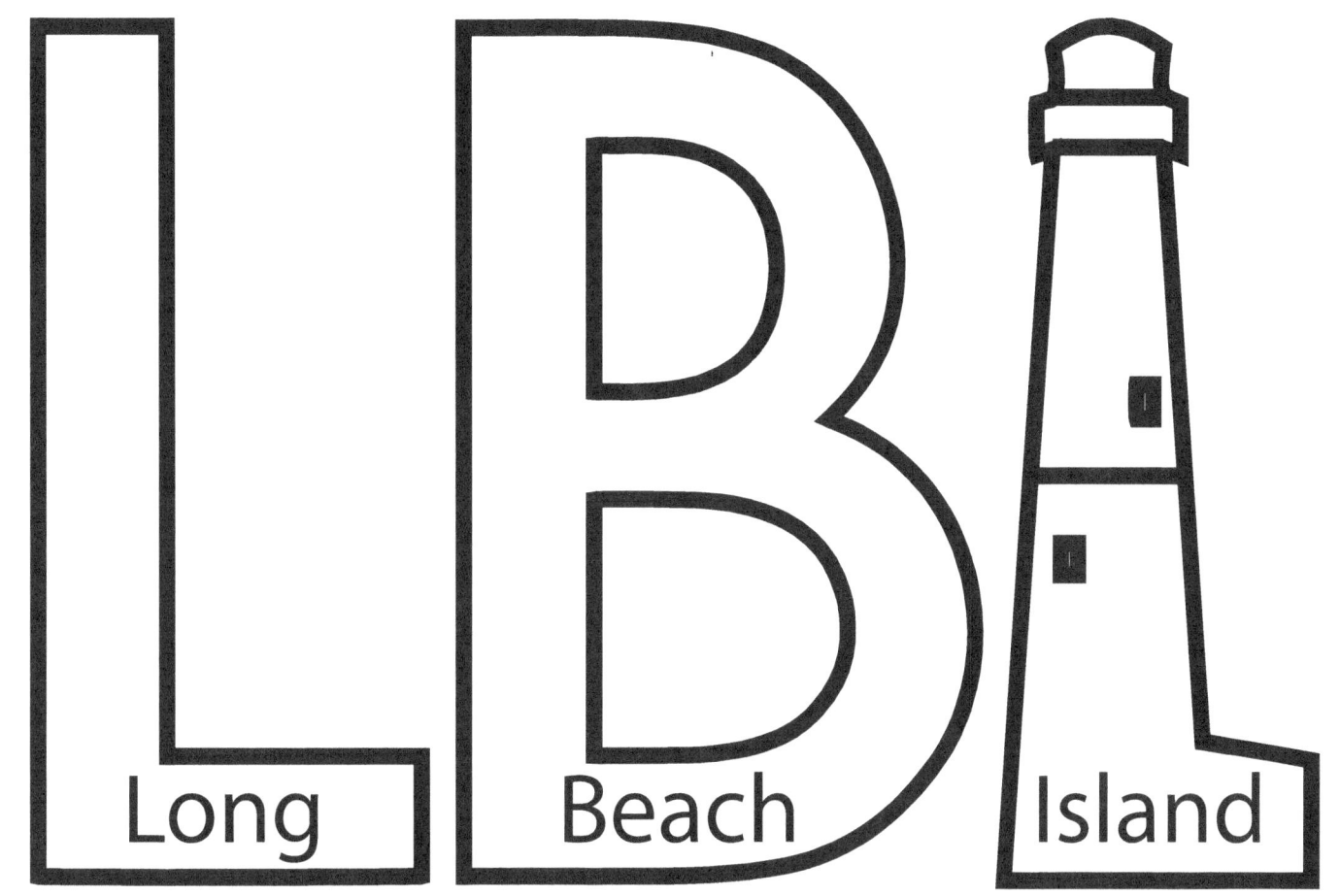

Long Beach Island

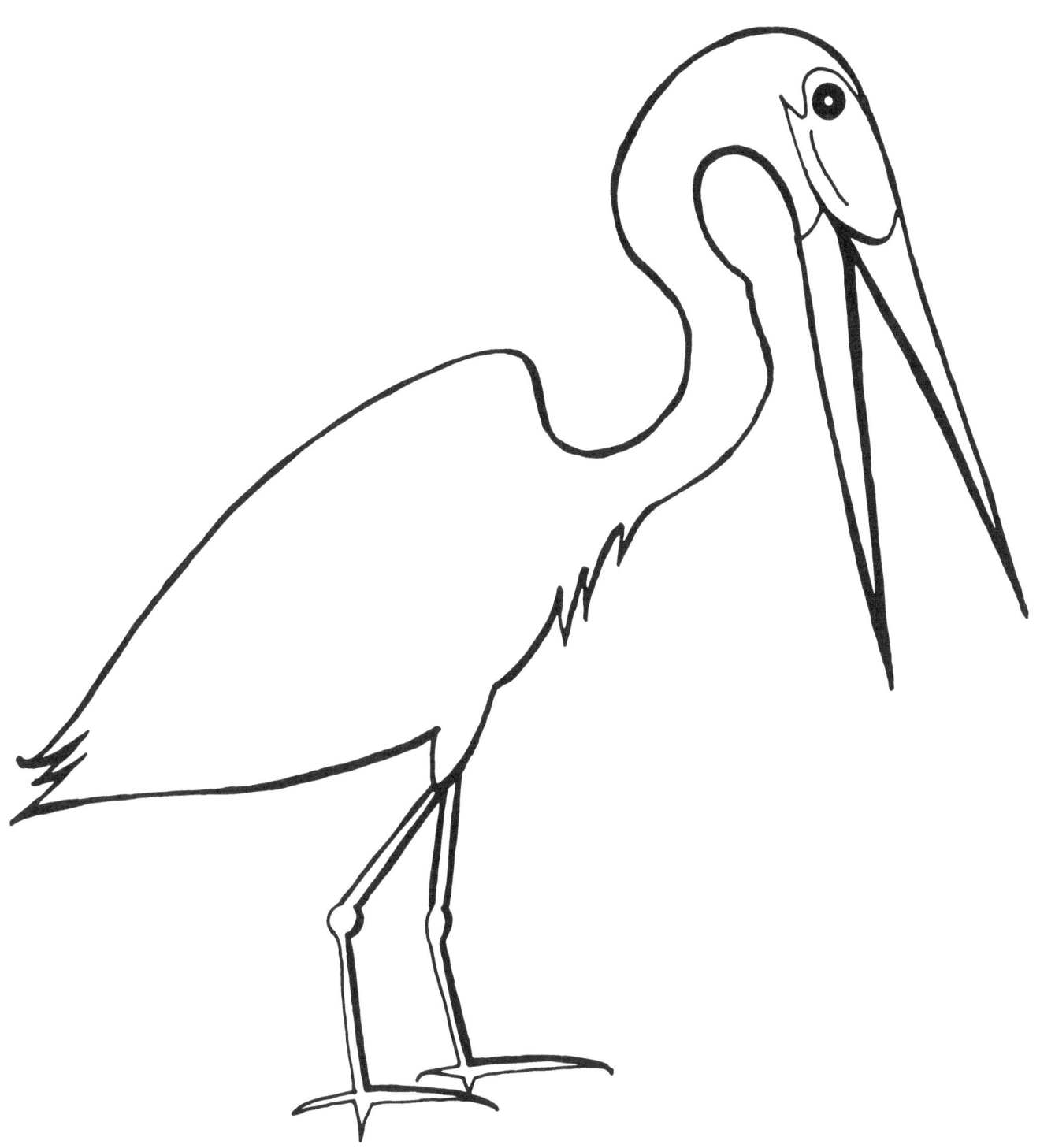

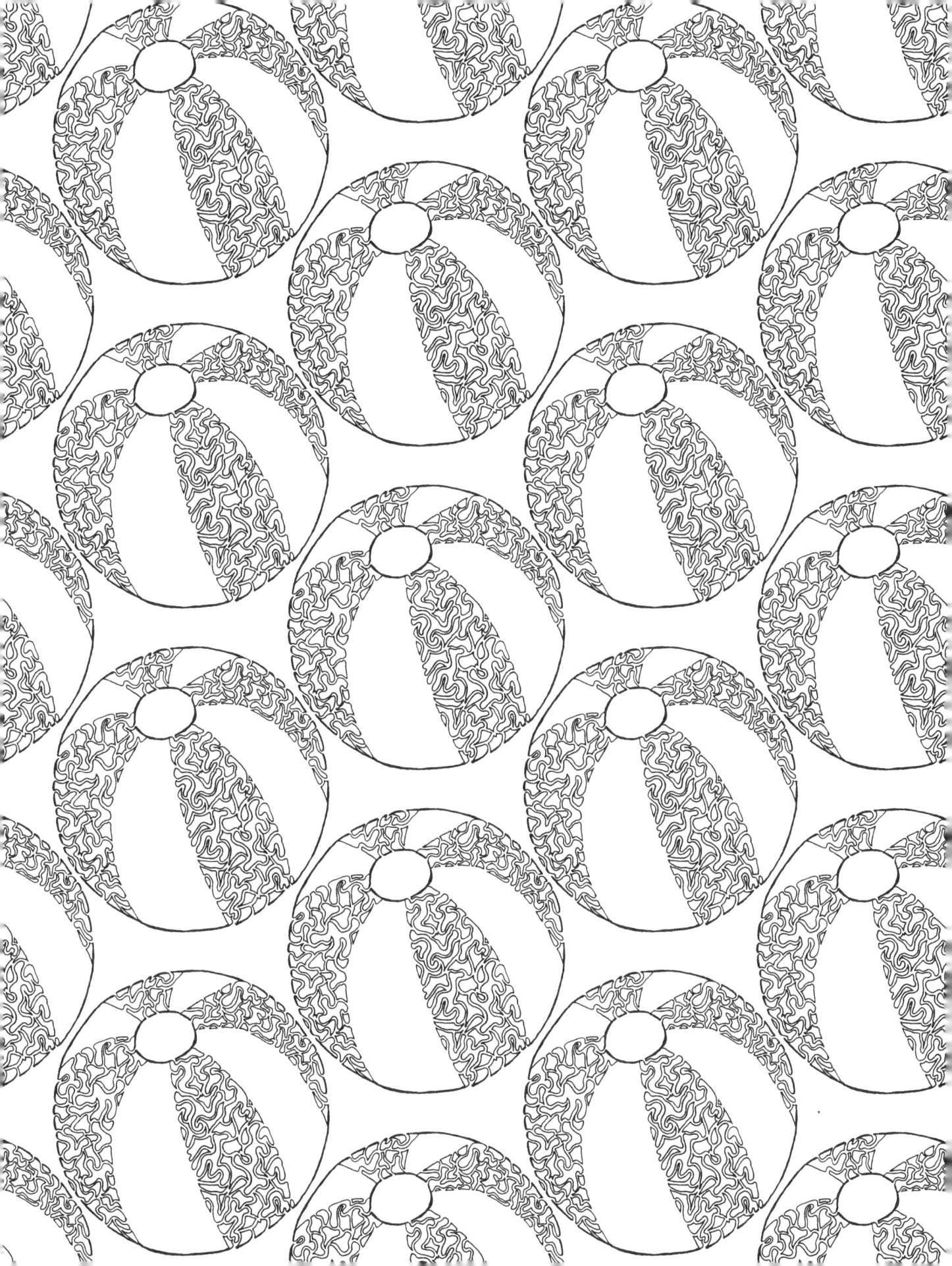

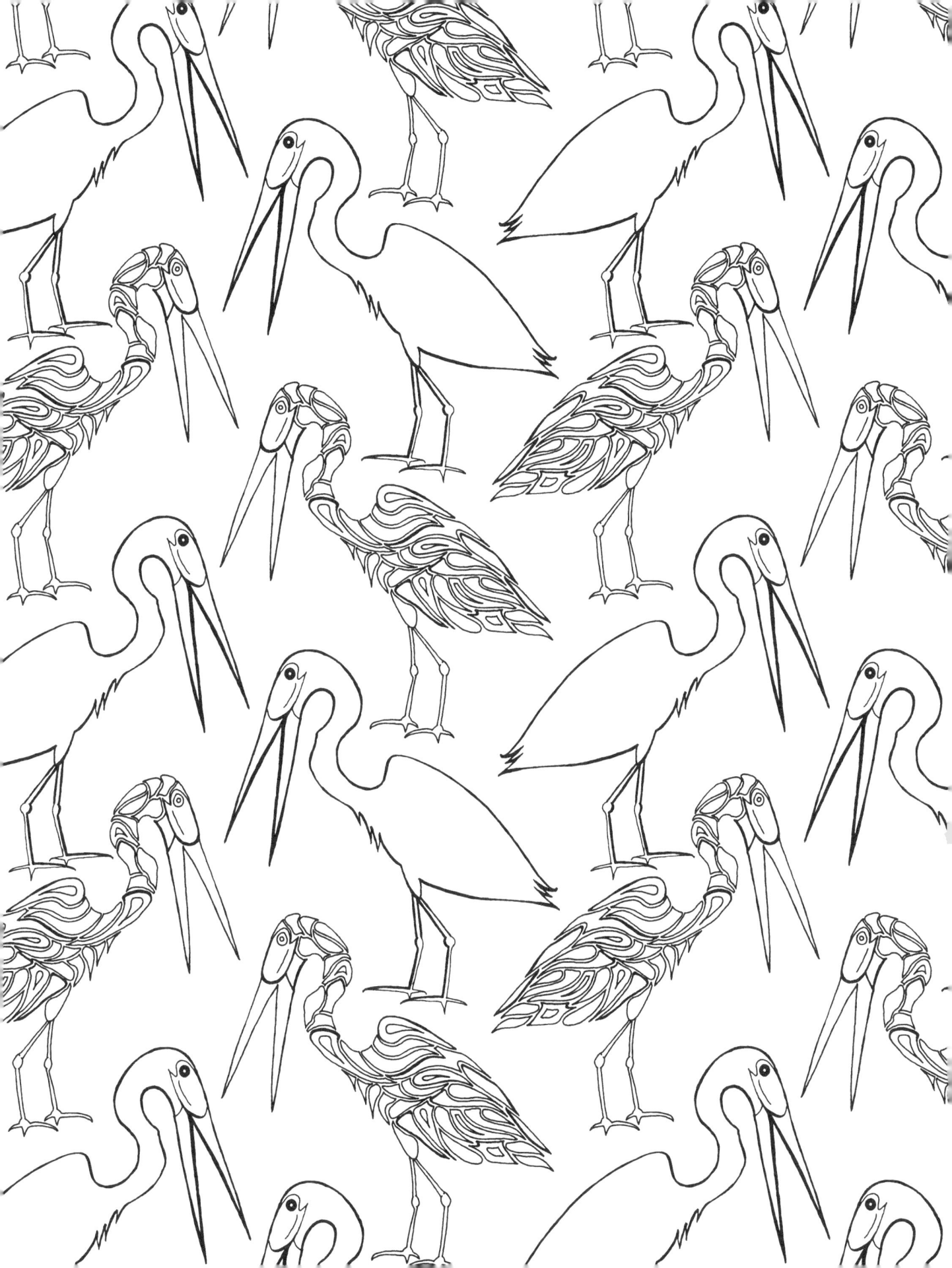

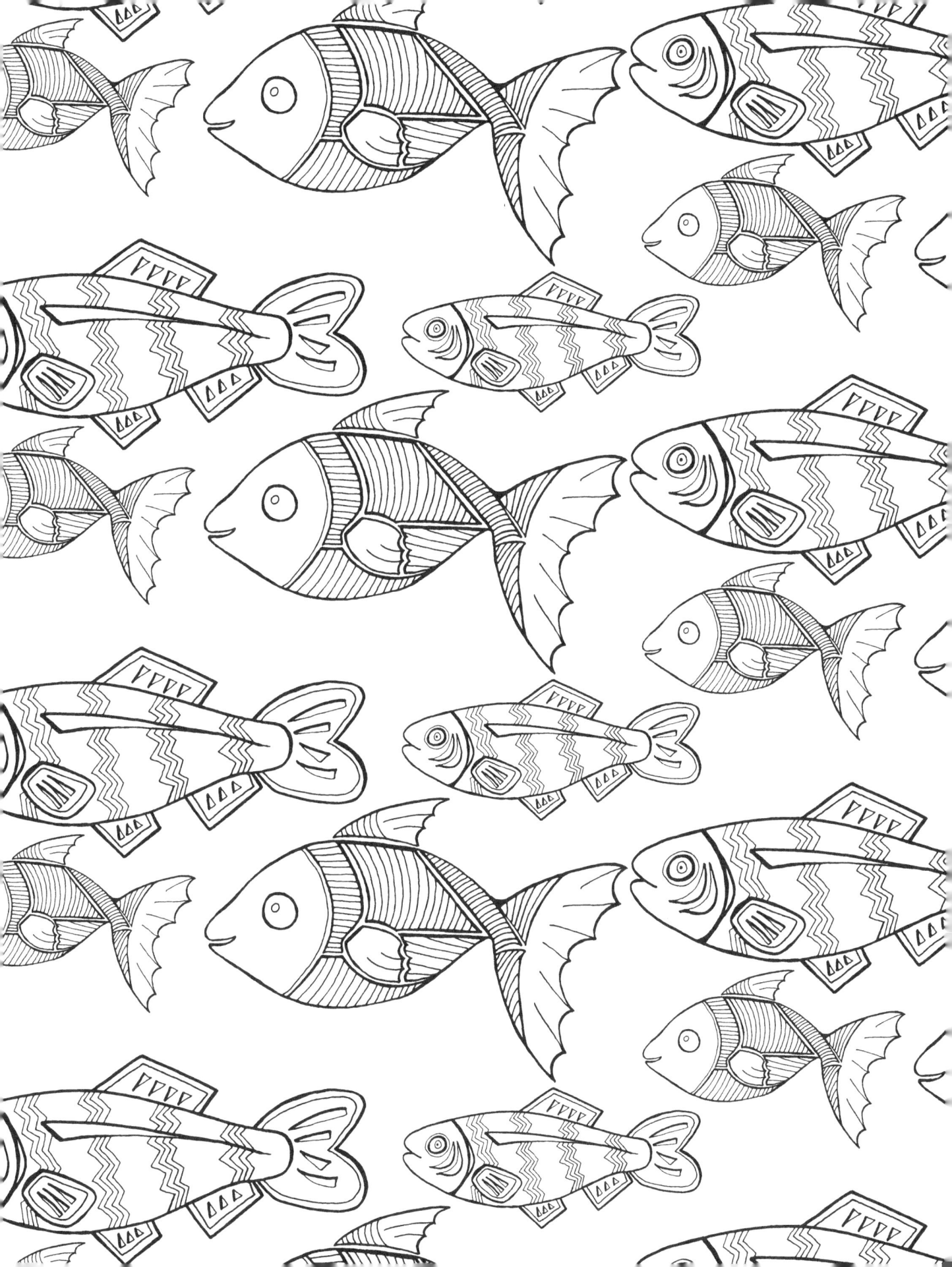

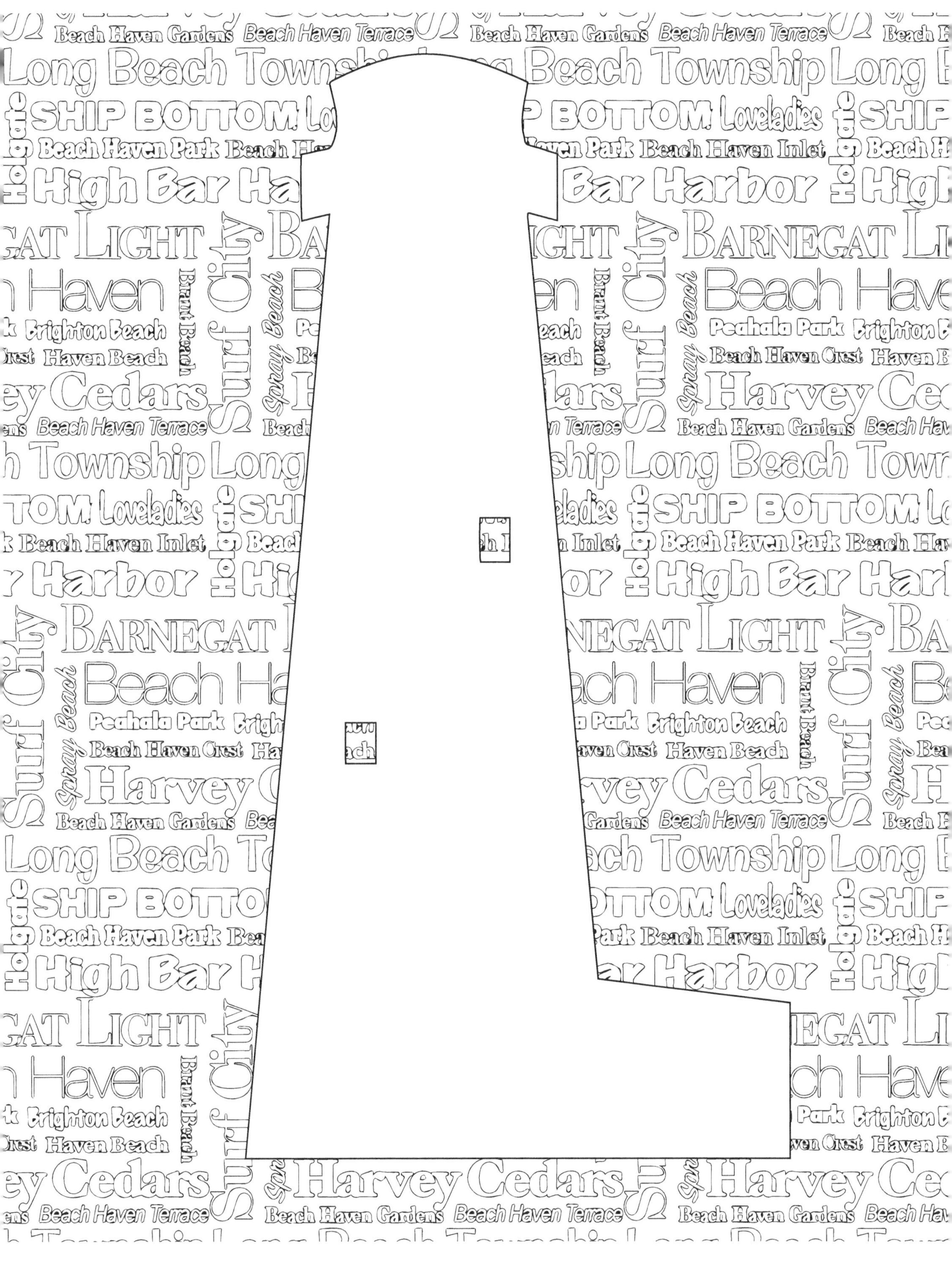

Samples from other **Coloring For Life** coloring books

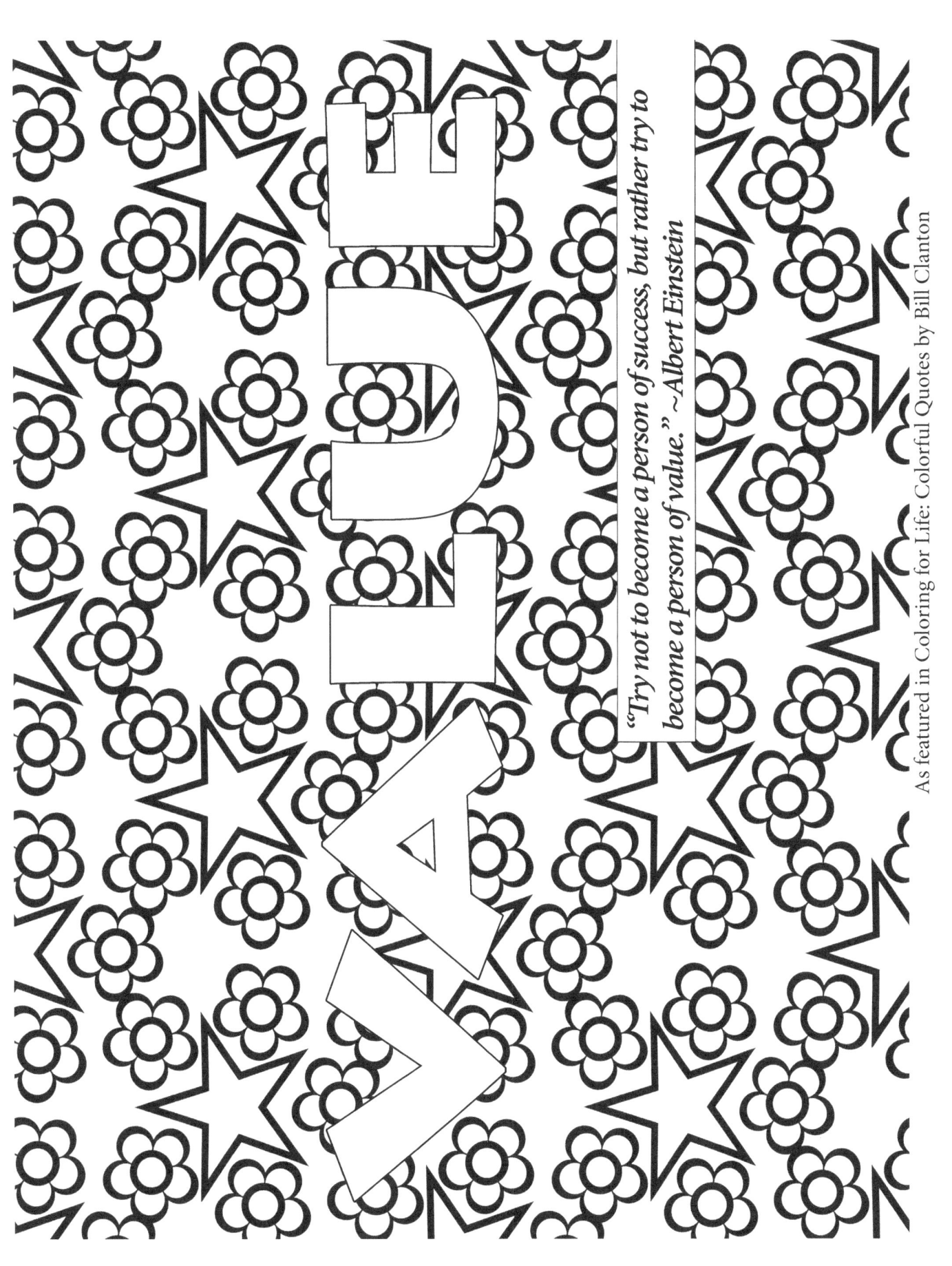

"Try not to become a person of success, but rather try to become a person of value." ~Albert Einstein

As featured in Coloring for Life: Colorful Quotes by Bill Clanton

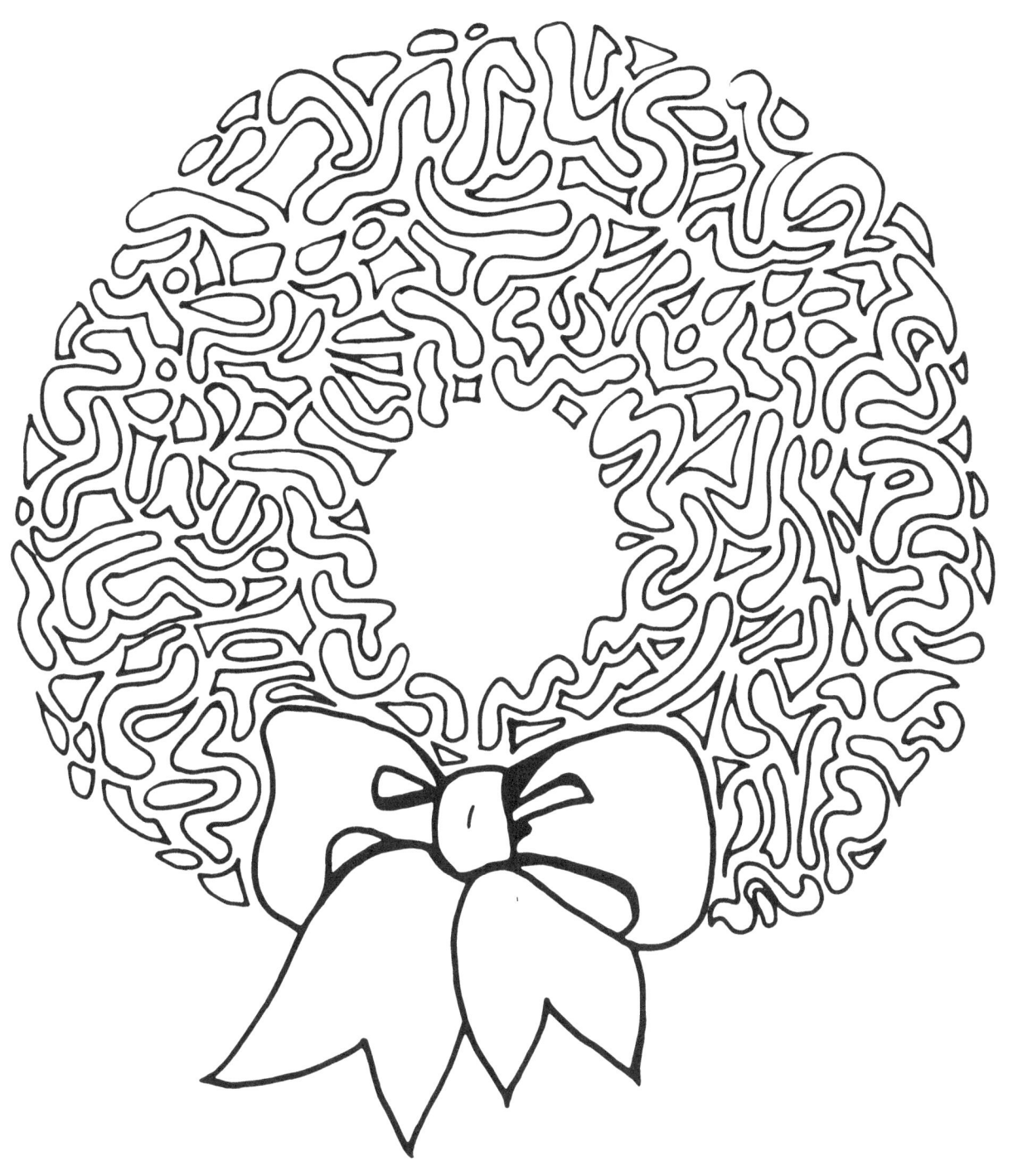

As featured in Coloring for Life: Colorful Christmas by Bill Clanton

Thank You

If you enjoyed this book, please look for Bill Clanton's other coloring books.

Coloring for Life: Colorful Quotes
- ISBN-13: 978-0-9974996-0-5

Coloring for Life: Colorful Christmas
- ISBN-13: 978-0-9974996-1-2

Coloring for Life: Colorful Coast
- ISBN-13: 978-0-9974996-2-9

Coloring for Life: Colorful Coast (Long Beach Island Edition)
- ISBN-13: 978-0-9974996-3-6

Coloring for Life: Colorful Coast (Cape May, NJ Edition)
- ISBN-13: 978-0-9974996-4-3

If you've ever considered making your own coloring book for grown ups, look for Bill Clanton's guide outlining the steps necessary to get your book published.

Creating a Coloring Book for Adults: Learn the Secrets to Getting Your Coloring Book Published

Kindle:
ASIN: B0194D3Gl6

Paperback:
- ISBN-10: 1519761872
- ISBN-13: 978-1519761873

We hope you've enjoyed this coloring book. Please take a moment to share your work on social media with the hashtag #coloringforlife.

Web: coloringforlife.com
Twitter: twitter.com/coloringforlife
Facebook: facebook.com/coloringforlife
Coloring for Life 2016

Sign up for our newsletter at coloringforlife.com and receive free coloring pages and updates on future Coloring for Life coloring books.

www.ingramcontent.com/pod-product-compliance
Lightning Source LLC
Chambersburg PA
CBHW080949170526
45158CB00008B/2420